DON'T CALL ME CHRISTIAN

Paul Liberman & Jack Wasson

TISHBITE PRESS

DON'T CALL ME CHRISTIAN
by Paul Liberman and Jack Wasson

Published by Tishbite Press
3030 Matlock Road, Suite #201
Arlington, TX 76015

Books may be ordered through book website
www.DontCallMeChristian.com and through most major book
distributors.

Cover Design by Jack Wasson and Daniel Savart

Visit author's website at www.JacobReport.com

Library of Congress Control Number: 2015905130

ISBN 10-digit: 0692419365
ISBN 13-digit: 978-0692419366

First edition

14 15 16 17 18 – 9 8 7 6 5 4 3 2 1
Printed in the United States of America

Dedication

This book is dedicated to Susan; my best friend, partner, and the love of my life. Thank you, dear, for 50 great years.

Paul Liberman,
February, 2015

Table of Contents

Foreword—The Story Behind the Story

By Jack Wasson

When I first approached Paul Liberman with doing "his story," he was reluctant to say the least. As I already knew, Paul is averse to anything that can be considered "self-promotion" or "self-glorification." I convinced Paul to sit down with me in his home and allow me to interview him with an MP3 digital recorder. I pointed out that, at a minimum, it could be a historical record for his grandchildren. That was the argument which sealed the deal. So we began to conduct a series of very personal interviews.

Before we finished the first day, I realized this was an extraordinary story which would be meaningful to a broad spectrum of readers. Not unexpectedly, Paul was surprised. *"I don't understand. What's so unusual about my story?"* He protested. *"It's a typical Jewish story!"*

I'm certain you will agree with me that although there are many aspects of Paul's story which are "typically Jewish," there are many other aspects which are totally unique—at times even unbelievable.

For two girls raised in the White House, riding to school every day in a black SUV escorted by the Secret Service, might seem like an ordinary experience. However, the little girl who resides outside Omaha and waits with her little sister at the bus stop for the big yellow school bus might disagree. The point is, for every individual, their own life seems typical and it is only when contrasted to others that the dissimilarities become obvious. "Typical" is in the eyes of the beholder.

Some of this story is so unusual, the cover of the "pre-publication" manuscript carried the words, *"The True Story of Paul Liberman"* (my idea).

Foreword—The Story Behind The Story

Throughout this project, Paul and I have been very much in agreement, except for those words I proposed for the cover. My logic was that the world is full of fiction and fantasy. Alternative reality sells, even in the universe of religion and spiritual things. I thought it was important that we declare right on the cover that this is a true story. How many times have I gone to a movie with my wife and we've turned to one another at the same moment with the question, *"Is this a true story? Did this really happen?"*

However, Paul was averse, once again, because he believed the words might appear too much like self-promotion. I relented with regard to the cover; but, rest assured, every event and account in this book was scrutinized for accuracy. The account of Paul's grandfather is taken from personal conversations Bernard Liberman had with Paul during Paul's youth. It is as accurate as a recollection can be after sixty years.

I believe you will find this story as special as I did and will enjoy reading it as much as I enjoyed writing it.

The Past Is Prologue

My grandfather, Bernard Liberman, was born about 1894 in Minsk—the capital of Belarus. Belarus is a landlocked country in Eastern Europe bordered by Russia to the northeast, Ukraine to the south, Poland to the west, and Lithuania and Latvia to the northwest.

Within the Pale (the eastern territories and countries of the Czarist Empire, the "Russias," as they were known), Jewish education was a coveted commodity available only to a few, and especially limited amongst the poor, which included the Libermans. The lack of educational opportunities centered on the complicated circumstance of the Jews living under the Czar's government.

For example, law mandated that only one out of 10 children in public schools could be Jewish. This was one of the Czar's measures employed to keep the Jews from becoming "too powerful" and exploiting the Christian majority population.

Wealthier Jews circumvented the law by paying for nine Gentile children to attend school in order that there would be a single opening for their own child. But, the poorer Jewish families lacked that option. The only alternative was a rabbinic education.

Bernard Liberman was the oldest son, and as was customary for the oldest son, he was in training to become a rabbi. One benefit of this training included education in reading and writing so the students could study the Talmud and other historic and traditional rabbinic literature. My grandfather was the only one in his family who could read—also not unusual. His classes were all provided through the synagogue school—the *Cheder*. An added benefit of his rabbinic studies was the opportunity to sleep on a bench at the synagogue. With seven kids in the Liberman family, this was not a small subsidy.

The Past is Prologue

As the Twentieth century began, there were constant attacks on the Jewish population that lived in the Pale. This was nothing new. There had been centuries of hostility toward the Jews of Europe as far back as biblical times.

The roots of this hostility—or anti-Semitism—are disputed. My own opinion is that answers are located in the history of Europe. Without dispute, anti-Jewish antagonisms accompanied the spread of Christianity throughout the continent.

For centuries, literacy was the currency of wealth and power, and the Catholic Church was the bastion of European learning. Those who rose to prominence were primarily educated in the Church, or in church schools. Ostensibly, the foundation of this education was the Bible. Early on in the history of the Catholic Church, the Jews became identified with those who resisted God. With large populations of illiterate citizens looking for answers for every plague, drought, or famine, Church leaders pointed with authority to the Bible.

The "rejecters," or "Christ-killers," were presumed to be at the source of every problem. Of course, not only was the largest majority of the

> The two religions had thus emerged as foes—rival claimants to the same inheritance and the same legacy.

Christian population illiterate—unable to read or write—in German, French, or later Russian, but the "authority" of the Church was contained in a separate, dead language—Latin. It wasn't enough that the population couldn't read their own language; the Scriptures were in *"code,"* a code only those trained in the Church could read, speak, and write—or interpret.

Parallel to the development and expansion of the Christian Church through Catholicism, the European Jewish communities developed and maintained their own separate educational systems that also orbited around the Bible (as well as the rabbinic traditions). Unwelcome within the Christian communities and centers of education, Jews learned early on to disengage from their surrounding neighbors, even evolving a separate language—Yiddish. Therefore, reading and writing revolved around Latin and the Church amongst the Christian population, and Hebrew and Yiddish in the Jewish communities.

Christians worshiped the Jewish God and based their faith on Jewish scriptures, but they largely rejected Jewish law, Judaic ritual, and Jewish nationhood. They claimed that Jesus Christ, the "son" of the Jewish God, had instituted a new covenant and a simplified set of standards that superseded the complex Judaic laws and customs. They asserted that Christianity had thus replaced Judaism as the true faith, and sometimes implied, and often stated outright, that Christians rather than Jews were now the "chosen people" and the new "Israel." The continued existence of the Jewish faith, however, and the refusal of most Jews to accept Christianity, cast some doubt on the validity of these claims, and implicitly challenged Christian credibility (and Church authority).[1]

The two religions had thus emerged as foes—rival claimants to the same inheritance and the same legacy. Early Christian writings tended to portray the Jews as a perfidious people who had rejected God's love, turned their back on God's salvation, and murdered God's son. The destruction of the Jewish state, the dispersion of the Jewish people, and the sufferings and persecutions inflicted upon the Jews were frequently cited as evidence of God's displeasure. In this tradition, the Jews became not just the rivals of Christianity, but the enemies of God himself.[2]

Centuries before my grandfather was born, in an effort to avoid persecution and improve their economic opportunities, thousands of Jews from Central Europe moved to the territories under Polish and Lithuanian control. Here, they had found something of a sanctuary. Although the Jews in Poland and

Lithuania were periodically subjected to indignities and persecutions, they were also protected at various times and in different ways by certain of the monarchs and the nobility. Jews performed valuable services for the crown, the landlords, and the economy—and all the while the Jewish community grew and flourished. By the sixteenth century, the Polish-Lithuanian lands had become the main homeland of European Jewry.[3]

The services Jews performed for the crown and nobility, however, were hardly designed to make them popular with the Christian masses. In rural areas, many Jews made their living as leaseholders—renting from their Polish landlords the rights to run farmlands, mills, dairies, orchards, taverns, and various other enterprises; and as tax collectors, financial agents, liquor dealers, and estate managers. In other words they were used as middlemen by lords and rulers to extract money from and supervise the affairs of the Christian peasants, and they thus attracted much of the contempt and resentment attached to such activities. In the towns where the Jews worked as merchants and craftsmen, they were often disliked and feared by their Christian counterparts who tended to view them as unwelcome outsiders and dangerous, industrious competitors. Such fears and resentments, as often as not, were reinforced by the anti-Judaic sentiments of the Christian church and its clergy. The Jews were widely seen as aliens, parasites, and exploiters—the purveyors of drunkenness, poverty, and immorality among the Christian people.[4]

Czarist Russia was historically isolated from the rest of Europe. It developed its own "approach," which invariably included a peculiarly Russian xenophobia—fear of foreigners. For centuries, the Russians harbored and instilled in the native populations the fear and threat of outsiders. Always aligned with and supported by the Russian Orthodox Church, successive Czarist governments perpetuated anti-Jewish sentiments, making Jews the ultimate "outsiders" and "foreigners." Initially, this was mostly a "theoretical" distrust of the Jews. Few Jews actually lived in

Russia proper. In the 19th century, Czarist governments supplanted the ruling Polish monarchs and much of the Turkish territories. With these subjugations, Russia "inherited" many thousands of Jews.

With this development, the anti-Jewish sentiment was no longer theoretical for the Russians. Many "temporary" measures and decrees were instituted in these newly acquired territories of Eastern Europe. All of the measures were designed to keep Russia safe from the corrupting impact of the foreign, Jewish influence. This was a policy of containment.

> Jews were strictly forbidden to travel "beyond the Pale"—the Eastern provinces—into the heartland of Russia.

For example, Jews were strictly forbidden to travel "beyond the Pale"—the Eastern provinces—into the heartland of Russia. Violation could result in capital punishment. The creation of the Pale, which came to be the foremost symbol of anti-Jewish discrimination, was in many respects an attempt to preserve the conditions that existed prior to the Russian expansion.

Educational measures were instituted limiting and even forbidding the education of Jewish children, further insulating and isolating the Jewish population. Many of the measures not only forbad Jews from entering "Mother Russia" but required entire communities of previously urban Jews to find "productive" work as rural farmers. Conversely, at times land was withheld and forbidden to Jewish landowners in an effort to protect the Christian populations from "exploitation." The sum total of these ongoing measures had the effect of reducing the majority of Eastern European Jews to abject poverty, making them unable to freely move about, to engage in a trade, or to educate their children.

[1]James Parkes, *Antisemitism* (Chicago: Quadrangle Books, 1963), pp. 60-62; Dennis Prager and Joseph Telushkin, *Why the Jews? The Reason for Antisemitism* (New York: Simon and Schuster, 1983), pp. 90-93; Edward H. Judge, *Easter in Kishinev— Anatomy of a Pogrom* (New York and London: New York University Press, 1992), p. 3.

[2]Edward H. Flannery, *The Anguish of the Jews: Twenty-three Centuries of Antisemitism* (New York: Paulist Press, 1985), pp. 28-46; Paul E. Grosser and Edwin G. Halperin, *Anti-Semitism: Causes and Effects* (New York: Philosophical Library, 1983), pp. 49-54; Jules Isaac, *The Teaching of Contempt: Christian Roots of Anti-Semitism* (New York: Holt, Rinehart and Winston, 1964), pp. 39-52; Judge, p. 3.

[3]Bernard D. Weinryb, *The Jews of Poland: A Social and Economic History of the Jewish Community in Poland from 1100 to 1800* (Philadelphia: Jewish Publication Society of America, 1972), pp. 24-30, 32-39, 41-48; John D. Klier, *Russia Gathers Her Jews: The Origins of the "Jewish Question" in Russia, 1772-1825* (De Kalb: Northern Illinois University Press, 1986) pp. 4-8; Judge, p. 6.

[4]Israel Friedlander, *The Jews of Russia and Poland* (New York and London: G. P Putnam's Sons, 1915), pp. 42-54; Klier, pp. 8-11; Weinryb, pp. 41-48; 56-70; Judge, p. 6.

1—Welcome to America

At the beginning of the 20th Century, the overt hostility of the Christian majority in Russia led many Jewish men, such as my grandfather's father, to emigrate. They were looking for better financial opportunities for themselves and their families. As was the case of my grandfather's father, these men frequently left their wives and children behind with a promise to *"send for them"* once gainful employment had been obtained. The reality was, many of these men *never* sent for their families. Instead they abandoned their wives and children, starting new families in America or wherever they ended up.

Sometime before the turn of the new century, Naftal Herschel Liberman, my grandfather's father, left from Minsk, Belarus, bound for the United States to obtain work. Because they could only afford a single passage, he traveled alone.

Naftal ended up in New York City while his wife, Hessie Freed Leiberman, my great-grandmother, was left with the seven children. A couple of years passed and the oldest child, Bernard, my grandfather who was 12 at the time, began to greatly miss his father. So, Bernard concocted a plan. He would write his mother a letter, forge his father's signature, and put it in the mailbox. Since Bernard was the only one who could read or write, no one could question his "official" letter, which said, *"I am in New York and I want you to come."*

Of course, they took Bernard's word for it. After all, he had read the letter to them! The plan worked. *"Finally we can come!"* So, the entire clan packed up and embarked for New York City.

As my grandfather was the oldest son and his father was gone, plus the fact that he was the only one who could read or write, at 12 years old Bernard was the uncontested head of the Liberman expedition that made its way from Minsk to New York City.

Somehow, they made the voyage by ship and landed in Boston, where many other new European immigrants first entered America. My grandfather was the spokesman for the newly arrived tribe from Russia. When the government official asked for the names of each of the passengers and heard "Liberman" the official started to write "L-i-e-berman," but my grandfather corrected him!

"In Russian you spell it L-i-b-e-r-m-a-n." In Russian, phonetically, an "I" is an "E." That is the reason we have always spelled our last name Liberman—because of that first experience of my Grandfather Bernard with the government civil servant.

"Oh, you're Jewish. The Jewish neighborhoods are over there!"

Hessie had the address where Naftal lived in some ethnic New York City neighborhood. Somehow, Hessie, Bernard and the clan obtained directions and made their way to the address in New York City, arriving with all their earthly belongings—everything the eight of them could carry! One day they just showed up at the door. *"Hello, we're here!"*

I'm sure this was quite a shock! I can imagine Naftal's face. *"You asked for us to come and here we are!"* To say he was flabbergasted would be an understatement. But, it was done. There was no turning back now.

That's how the Libermans immigrated to the United States. If it hadn't been for 12-year-old Bernard Liberman, my grandfather, our history would certainly have taken an entirely different direction.

Now Naftal had to get busy supporting an additional eight people—a wife and seven children. Remember, my grandfather, Bernard, was the only one who could read or write. Certainly, none of them could speak a word of English!

Time passed, and, of course, the Libermans were living in an immigrant Jewish neighborhood. Like so many others before them, the goal of the trip was to get to America. Once they arrived, the first place they saw was New York City. *"Oh, you're Jewish. The Jewish neighborhoods are over there!"* Naturally, they would gravitate to those who also spoke Yiddish, which was their language. Everyone had to do their part to try and help pay the bills.

Time passed, and Bernard was a teenager. He worked hard to gain employment. His only education was his early rabbinic training back in Minsk. He could barely speak English. He could read and write in Hebrew and Yiddish, but that didn't create a lot of opportunities. However, he made his way with odd jobs—anything to contribute. Eventually, when he was 17 or 18 years old, he obtained a job making and fixing jewelry. The thing was, in order to get all of his work done, sometimes the job required Bernard to work on Saturday—the Shabbat.

> Naftal tore his lapel, the Jewish custom upon hearing of the death of a close family member.

One Saturday, Bernard rushed home to join in the Shabbat activities after putting in time helping to support the family. In his rush to get home, he neglected to notice the *dust* on his shoes—from the refining of jewelry! He came home, and his father noted his shoes. It did not look like regular dust, but *another* kind of dust. Naftal knew what it was and that my grandfather *had been working—on Shabbat!* So Naftal confronted my grandfather, *"What is this about? It's Shabbat!"*

Naftal didn't even stop to consider what my grandfather was trying to do—to get and keep a career to help support the rather large Liberman family. My grandfather confessed he had been working on Saturday. *"I've got to have a job and that's what they required of me."*

1—Welcome to America

At that point, Naftal tore his lapel, the Jewish custom upon hearing of the death of a close family member. Then he shouted, *"You're dead to me now. You've broken the Shabbat. Leave my home! I never want to see you again!"*

My grandfather loved his father and he would have done anything to please him. His father's outburst must certainly have broken my grandfather's heart, but he was told to leave so he left without protest.

Now, he was dead to his entire family: father, mother, sisters and brothers.

2—The Family Business

Bernard was on his own.

Employment was always difficult for the new immigrant Jews. First, there was the language problem. Few could speak English, and if they could, it was frequently with a heavy accent. There was no minimum wage or unemployment compensation. If you were the Jewish guy, you were always expendable. The Jews were the last ones hired and the first ones fired. There was also a lot of prejudice in those days. It was normal for the classified ads to specify, *"Good Christian man a must."* This really meant, *"No Jews need apply!"*

Shortly after he had been declared dead by his father, Bernard was once again unemployed. Even when my grandfather had work, he was chronically *losing* his job. But, at least then with his family, he had a place to stay. Now he was on his own. This was the situation when he found himself sitting on a New York City park bench wondering, *'What am I going to do? Where am I going to go now?'*

It was a windy day. A sheet out of a newspaper flew by. It was the classifieds—the want ads. By this time, Bernard could read English, and he took note that it was a Chicago newspaper. He casually read the ads because he had nothing better to do.

That is when Bernard saw an advertisement for someone who could do jewelry work. He was trained to do this, so he thought, *'Why not? I have nothing and no one left in New York.'* Bernard had only the clothes he was wearing. There was nothing to pack. Then and there, he struck out for Chicago with the ad folded up in his pocket.

Bernard journeyed all the way to Chicago to answer the ad. It never occurred to him that, by the time he got there, the job could have been filled! He took the chance, and they hired him! That's how the Liberman family wound up in Chicago.

By day, Bernard was working on his new jewelry job in Chicago. One evening, at a party, a really cute American Jewish girl caught his eye, so he decided to invite her out to a party. Her name was Nettie.

The night came for their big first date. At the party, everyone was singing around a piano when Nettie turned to Bernard. *"You can't sing at all!"* Even so, he was definitely taken with her and, not long after they first met, they were married *in spite of* what she thought of his singing. But my grandfather was so devastated by Nettie's criticism that, even after they got married, for the rest of his life, he would never sing another song.

> It was normal for the classified ads to specify, *"Good Christian man a must."* This really meant, *"No Jews need apply!"*

Bernard continued to struggle to stay employed. After his experience with his father, he wouldn't be involved in a synagogue, but he was always part of the Jewish community. All Jewish people spoke Yiddish, and that made you a member of the club. In those days, you *had* to speak Yiddish just to get by. The Jews came to America from countless European nations, yet everyone spoke the same language—*Yiddish*. It was a strong unifying factor. Sometimes, you could even get employment through contacts within the Yiddish community.

My Grandfather was bouncing around, trying to stay employed, scrambling to make a living. Then, through one of his Yiddish contacts, maybe at a party or something, he heard that electricity was coming to Chicago in a big way. He also heard it was going to be a growing industry for the future. He understood that, if he were an electrician, there would be lots of opportunities. It was the equivalent of high tech today.

Right before World War I, electricity was really starting to catch on. After Edison invented the light bulb, there was a scramble to capture the most lucrative markets. Most of the growth was in New York City and Chicago. This was because the transmission lines had to be very close to the turbines that made the electricity—as close as one mile. To make it commercially viable, the producers of electricity needed as many potential customers for their product as they could find within a short distance. The densest population clusters were in New York City and Chicago. By 1870, Chicago was the second largest city in the United States.

During the first decades of the 20th century, there was a lot of mystery surrounding the entire electrical industry. This was further compounded because there was a competition between two types of electricity: DC (Direct Current) and AC (Alternating Current). Edison, the inventor of the light bulb plus numerous electrical appliances, bet heavily on DC. His major competition was George Westinghouse who promoted AC. The feud frequently spilled over into the public. Newspapers wrote stories about this "novel" new invention. Each side was quick to condemn the other system and played frequently on the public's safety concerns. The invention of the electric chair and its use in lieu of hanging proved to everyone that "electricity can kill."

Very shortly after first hearing about electricity, my grandfather quickly found work in the electrical field. Nobody knew anything about electricity, so he wasn't behind. One

He soon discovered a lot of people wouldn't buy from a Jew, and a lot of people wouldn't sell to a Jew.

time, he was carrying in a coil of armored cable—BX. He laid the coil of wire on the floor where he was working, and the woman customer told her children, *"You have to go into the other room while he's working. I don't want you to get hurt with this. Just don't go anywhere near that coil of wire."* That's how much people knew about electricity.

2—The Family Business

It was 1915. Bernard was in his early 20s when he began working for an electrician, learning everything he could about the business. My grandfather and his boss were buying supplies, buying supplies, buying supplies—until they ran out of money. Now what were they supposed to do? They had no more cash. The solution: They took the supplies and sold them. They sold the inventory. That was easy because there was a lot of demand for electrical supplies.

They couldn't get electrical work, but they could sell off their inventory. My grandfather and his employer concluded that was the business they would go into—selling electrical materials and supplies. Bernard became partners with the man who had hired him.

The new partners began the business in 1915. Bernard continued in the electrical supply business. After that, he never again had to look for another job. There were always enough buyers for electrical materials to stay in business. After a few years, my grandfather bought out his partner for $100.00 and then *he* owned the business. By that time, he was married to Nettie, and they had two sons. Marvin, my father, was born in 1918, and Harold, his brother, arrived in 1925.

The electrical field was growing, and now Bernard had work. However, he soon discovered a lot of people wouldn't buy from a Jew, and a lot of people wouldn't sell to a Jew. His English was poor, and he could hardly write. If you're Jewish, not speaking English very well, and you can hardly write English, you've got a problem.

My grandfather struggled with the business, and then came the Depression. He struggled, but he was only making $8.00 a week. That didn't leave any money for heat. My grandmother used to wake up in the apartment with the water by her bed frozen. That's how cold it was in Chicago.

2—The Family Business

The Depression was under way and the creditors were closing in. My grandfather was barely scraping by. In Illinois, it took three people to force an involuntary bankruptcy. Two of his creditors signed for the filing, and the third one was about to sign to file. Bernard knew that the next day the third guy was going to sign the papers and he would be officially bankrupt and out of business.

My grandfather was broke and he owed everybody money. He couldn't sleep because the next day was the end. About 3:00 a.m. in the morning, he came up with an idea. He immediately called the third guy who was supposed to sign the next day. *"I'll pay you everything I owe you if you meet me at my place now, within the hour."*

My grandfather told him to come by at 6:00 a.m. The creditor was willing to do *anything* to get paid, so he came over. My grandfather got there early. He took a great big sheet of brown wrapping paper and all of his inventory "dogs"—all the inventory items he couldn't sell—and wrapped them up. Then he went to the catalog and found all the catalog numbers for these items. Whatever the book value was, he listed it and showed it with the catalog number and the price from the catalog, so that it could be proven. He listed all of this on a sheet of paper. Then, he packed the items in boxes.

The fellow was so grateful! My grandfather gave him a copy of his bill and told him to mark it, *"Paid in full."* The guy gladly complied with his signature and the date. Then the man took the boxes full of the inventory dogs and left. Needless to say, the other two creditors who had already signed the bankruptcy paperwork were furious. Their attitude was, *"You dummy!"* But it was too late. That's how the family electrical supply business survived and escaped bankruptcy during the Great Depression.

In 1934, my father, Marvin, was 16 years old. He was a regular American teenager who attended public school in Chicago. Naturally, he could read, write and speak English like a native. My grandfather, Bernard, became very reliant on my father, especially in the business. In fact, the entire family was very dependent on my father. That made my father the knowledgeable person.

My grandfather did all the physical work of the business, and my father did all the paperwork. My father was always a man of common sense. It was a small family business with an uncertain future. Now it was going to continue because of my father.

My father and Sylvia Schreiber, my mother, first met when they were 14 years old. They were sweethearts all through high school. At my grandfather's urging, they finally married on my father's 22nd birthday. It was 1940 and, to my Grandfather, it was obvious there was going to be a war. He couldn't afford to lose my father to the draft and keep the business running.

"Listen Marvin, you're probably going to marry Sylvia eventually anyhow. There's a war coming. We need for the two of you to get married. Perhaps the married men won't be drafted."

That's how it happened that, in 1940, Marvin and Sylvia Liberman, my father and mother, were married. Even though Sylvia was his childhood sweetheart, my Dad probably would have just gone along and gone along. Who knows if he would ever have married her if his father hadn't pushed the issue?

After that, the war in Europe began. It was a small business and my grandfather was still concerned about losing my father to the war. That is when my grandfather said, *"Marvin, having children would also help to keep you out of the war. You should have children."* Sure enough, in 1941, my mother became pregnant with her first child, which was me—Paul Liberman.

I was born January 31, 1942, just eight weeks after Pearl Harbor. Then, my grandfather told my father, *"We have to get you another child, because one child may not keep you out of the war. You better have another one."* So, 18 months later, Dean, my younger brother was born and my father was out of the draft. In 1949 and 1951, my two brothers, Marc and Mitchell, were born.

2—The Family Business

My father was working in the Liberman electrical company, which was kind of a bumble-along business. However, it was enough to support the family. My father was very good with paperwork. He was a very good administrator. Then he learned about government priorities and how to do the paperwork, which was the key during the war years to getting the materials which the business sold. He sent someone to Sears and Montgomery Ward to sell electrical items. He told them, *"We'll package electrical supply kits for you."* Sears was based in Chicago. My family would sell the kits at or near cost or slightly above cost.

That wasn't how they really made money. My father had a right hand man, Lester Burger, who would take some of the merchandise and sell it on the black market. My father and Lester didn't really care what kind of margins they made from buying and selling at Sears and Montgomery Ward. The *real* money was in scraping off some of the inventory—not delivering all of it—and then selling it on the black market. During the war, electrical parts, materials and supplies were almost impossible to get. My father's right-hand man was a salesman who believed when the war was over, *"A lot of people are going to owe us a bunch, because we got them through the war with electrical supplies."* It worked.

3—*Aluf*–The Israeli General

During WWII, income tax rates ran as high as 90%. My father and grandfather, Bernard Liberman, developed a business and a customer base that helped them survive the war years. After the war ended, it really paid off. My grandfather was always a very hardworking man. He worked like a dog all the time, doing intense physical work.

In 1947, Bernard's entire body was falling apart. He had so many different maladies and diseases, he could hardly walk; a stomach condition and a heart condition. His entire body was breaking down and he was only 55 years old. It was because he was doing all of the manual labor for the family electrical supply business. That's when my father said, *"Dad, I'll buy you out of the business. I'll pay you over 20 years from the profits of the business. If you don't make it, I'll own the business outright."* Later, this deal was also amended to include my father's younger brother, Harold. After that, the two Liberman brothers owned the business together.

Bernard was certain his health was sinking fast. In 1947, he moved to Miami *to die*, or so he thought. All his life, he was used to working very hard. Now he had nothing to do and he was in Miami, waiting to die.

After the war, many wealthy Jews moved to Florida and retired to Miami Beach. They came from New York, Chicago and all over the East Coast. If you were Jewish and had money, you moved to Miami, Florida. At that time, they didn't know anything about Fort Lauderdale or Jacksonville.

In 1948, Bernard became absolutely captivated with a vision for the establishment of the State of Israel. Here was a man who was born and raised in czarist Russia. He was aware, firsthand, of the hostilities the Russian Jews experienced. Then all the reports came out about what the Nazis had done. Israel would be a place for the Jews to go—a place of our own. It really captured my grandfather's imagination.

Bernard felt that, with the remaining time he had left, he had to do everything he could—to devote his entire life and effort—to raising money for Israel. So, he volunteered for the *Combined Jewish Appeal, the Jewish Federation,* and all the Jewish charities, and they put him to work. He was a volunteer and he didn't cost them anything. He was receiving what amounted to a stipend from my father for the purchase price of the family electrical supply business.

Bernard was working full time, and then some, for the charities, helping to sell Israel bonds, and raising contributions. He made appointments with the wealthy Jewish people of Miami Beach and the other Jewish communities. He was only a volunteer, but his passion showed through, which meant he was able to raise a lot of money.

He worked more than full time, raising money for Israel during the period 1947–1980. Eventually, he had a whole wall in his living room filled with plaques and awards that he had been given over the years for raising money on behalf of Israel and the Jewish community. This was really important work.

After the nation of Israel was founded, my grandfather was invited to visit with David Ben-Gurion in Israel, at the State of Israel's expense. While in Israel, he would have dinner with Ben-Gurion. He was a celebrity of sorts, because he was the most successful fundraiser in all of Miami, Florida. Perhaps there were bigger fundraisers in New York, but my grandfather was definitely "somebody" in the eyes of David Ben-Gurion.

Ben-Gurion entertained Bernard in appreciation of the countless millions of dollars that he raised. No one really knew how much money he raised. It was clearly well beyond many tens of millions of dollars over all those years. Out of appreciation, the Knesset did a one-time, very special honor for my grandfather. The

Knesset passed a bill designating him an honorary *aluf.* Aluf is Hebrew for *"general."* My grandfather was made an honorary general in the IDF—*the Israeli Defense Forces*—for raising all of that money.

Golda Meir would invite political dignitaries for tea, but she invited my grandfather for dinner. He was really special in Israel. His immigrant experience fed his romance and dedication to the State of Israel.

All that time, Bernard thought he was dying, but he was just getting better. He was just keeping himself busy, but he was getting healthier all the time. Certainly, the early retirement was providential. It probably saved his life. My father and Uncle Harold had to pay him off. My grandfather made it the entire 20 years and then some. It wasn't that much money, but it was enough for him and my grandmother to live on. They lived very simply.

> Golda Meir would invite political dignitaries for tea, but she invited my grandfather for dinner.

For most of his life, my grandfather was separated from his family. Eventually, when he reached his 70s, he somehow reconnected with some of his brothers and sisters. However, they were scattered all over the country.

Once my grandfather stopped all the physical work, he began to recover his health. He worked on behalf of Israel until the end of his life. He lived to be 88 years old, and passed on in 1980.

4—"Jesus, Help Me!"

My father had his business in Chicago, and he was working very hard. He was always a common sense, upright man. He wasn't really an entrepreneur, but he was a very good administrator. Once my Grandfather was retired and in Miami, my father was in business with his brother, my Uncle Harold. Uncle Harold never cared that much for the electrical supply business, but it was a living. He did so out of respect for his father. Also, I don't believe he thought he could make as good a living doing anything else. That left it largely to my father to operate the business.

After the war there was a huge demand for electrical appliances, so they expanded the business to include electrical appliances. During the summer, before air conditioning, electric fans were also a big sales item. During the late 1940s and early 1950s, the business had ten good years. Then, sometime during 1955-56, the business began to lose money.

During the ten good years, my father had to share the profits with Uncle Harold. For the times, it was a comfortable living; but my family was certainly not wealthy. The Jewish neighborhood where we lived consisted mostly of small businessmen earning better than average incomes.

After ten lucrative years, my father continued to plug away. When the company began to lose money, the business had savings to fall back on. My father was sheltering the family from this; and as a boy, I was oblivious to such matters. He continued drawing a nice salary, using what they had saved during the good years. As far as I knew, my father's business was doing fine. He totally insulated the family from the details of the business difficulties.

Every summer, from my earliest years, starting at about the age of 12, I worked in the business. Everyone understood—we had a family business and it was expected. I worked in the shipping room lifting and working as a stock boy. At 16, I could drive and would make deliveries.

From then on, after school, I worked a 30-hour workweek. After school, I would take two buses to work. I arranged my schedule to get out at noon. Right away, I'd get on the bus. By 12:30 pm, I was at the business. We always worked at the store until 6:30 p.m. We also worked Saturday mornings, but I actually enjoyed it. Every day I worked making deliveries. I was learning the family business.

When I was a teenager, I was making a dollar an hour. I was the only kid who had bucks in his pocket, which made me feel great. I also saved some money. Then I turned 18, graduated from high school, and it was time to go to college.

The expected decision would have been to attend the University of Illinois, which was a little less expensive. It was $110 a semester for tuition versus $160 a semester at the University of Wisconsin. However, the University of Illinois was a Greek school—it had a lot of fraternities.

At my high school, we did pledging and paddled pledges. The idea was to humiliate the pledges as much as possible. For four years, I was in a high school fraternity and became the president of my fraternity. By my senior year, once I was through with the presidency, I had come to the conclusion the entire fraternity system was distasteful.

'What were we doing?' I recoiled from the entire idea of a fraternity. I had gone through it, and being the president was certainly great for dating. But, I made a decision. I didn't want to go to a Greek College campus. That's the reason I applied to the University of Wisconsin where fraternities were not such a big deal. There, it was possible to have a great social life *without* belonging to a fraternity.

Once I got to college, I worked at some menial jobs. All I had ever known was work. I felt very badly for my parents because of the cost of college. I waited tables in the girl's private dormitories, which turned out to be good for dating. I even washed dishes at the sorority houses; whatever it took to make some money. Then, I got a job going door-to-door selling jewelry at the girl's dormitories. I found different ways to earn money. Not only did I want to save my parents the expense of my college, but I also wanted some bucks in my pocket.

I had no idea that, back at home, things were drying up with the business. They weren't losing big money, but they were dipping into the savings to keep things going. Even though I didn't know, I felt the need to find work and take care of myself. That was when I started selling jewelry.

One day, a friend showed me a catalog that offered jewelry for sale. I tracked down the man behind the catalog. *"Look, I'll go door to door and I'll sell out of your catalog. I have the pictures of all the products. I'll buy from you wholesale. I'll book the orders, and you mail the product to them."* We struck a deal. Eventually, I started making some decent money. It worked out real well. I was making good money on the jewelry, plus I was meeting girls in the process.

Then I thought, *'I really need a car.'* I couldn't ask my parents for a car. That is when I decided, *'I'm going to go and buy the oldest wreck I can find. I'll fix it up so it runs really well. Then, I'll sell it.'* I knew a person could always get a little more money for a car on campus than in Chicago. The college students had never owned a car before, so you could charge a good price. That was also good for making a few bucks—the auto business.

I had the jewelry business, and I had the auto business. But, I was not a great student. At the end of my first semester, I called my father. *"Dad, I've gone to college. I've had the college experience. Now I think I want to quit. I want to get busy and make some money. You can't make any real money here."*

"Paul, I'm sorry to hear that. I certainly don't have much of a job for you. With no education, I don't know where you are going to find a job. These days, you need a college education." It was 1960 and I was 18 years old. What did I know?

He paused for a moment to let that all sink in, and then he said, *"You were driving a truck, and I think that is probably your future. You will drive a truck because that's all the education you have. I don't think anyone else can hire you beyond being a truck driver."* He was working on my head and it was effective. This was his way of encouraging me to stay in school. This little "talk" convinced me, so I remained in college.

I originally enrolled in Business Administration, but after a semester, I was on academic probation. After two semesters, I was on final probation. I wasn't even pulling a "C" average. This wasn't a great surprise, because I was never much of a student.

During my sophomore year, another student who was a friend of mine saw what was taking place. *"Look, Paul, you are going to flunk out. Your problem is that on registration day, you're just too ambitious for your own good. You haven't caught on. You pick courses based on what is going to be interesting, and how you're going to learn a lot and all those things. That's not what you should be doing. You should be doing what other people are doing—find the easy courses and sign up for those."*

Everything he said made sense. So, I asked him, *"Which ones are the easy courses?"*

Just like that, he gave me a list. I had to switch out of Business Administration, which had a lot of detailed work in accounting, mathematics, finance and statistics. I had been passing those courses, but not with good grades. That was my problem.

That list of "easy courses" saw me through the rest of my college career. In the process, I switched my major to Economics. From then on, I got As and Bs. Economics was very easy for me—loaded with big picture concepts. I could look at those charts and instantly, I knew what they meant. Nobody had to explain them to me. I could just look at the graph, and I would understand exactly what it was intended to convey.

When I came to my last semester at college, there was a course called *Money and Banking*. I had shown up during the first two weeks of the course and listened to the lectures. But, the professor never took attendance, and there was no midterm exam. The entire course grade was from a final exam. That left me thinking, *'No one knows if I'm here or not, right?'* I had other things to do on campus, plus it was my last semester.

I started cutting that class, and nobody noticed. Then, the time to drop a course and enroll in an alternative had come and gone. I was locked in. I had been part of the class for four weeks, but no one had seen me in two weeks. I thought the professor would certainly take note if I suddenly showed up because, by that time, the group had shrunk from 50 or 60 students down to 18. It was so small that it would be noticeable if somebody new abruptly appeared. Now, I was *afraid* to show up. This was really disturbing me. Then I began to worry. *'Maybe I'm not going to graduate.'*

It was coming down to the final exam. Everything rested on that test. I hadn't been to class since the second week. I was walking up the hill to class to take the exam, and I was feeling increasingly desperate. Then, I had a very unusual experience. In a single moment, out of the blue, I had a flashback—to something which had happened when I was 12 years old.

* * * * *

I was 12 years old, and it was around the time of Passover. During a service at our synagogue, I took note that, for some reason, the Passover Prayer Book had an English translation. Normally, our Siddur—our prayer book—contained only Hebrew. However, now there was a separate holiday prayer book with everything translated into English.

We were reading together the Hallel Psalms, in English, which made everything a lot easier to understand. I came to one of the Psalms, which says, *"The stone that the builders rejected has become the chief cornerstone."* I was reading this, when I thought to myself, *'Who was rejected by the fathers of the faith? The only one I can think of that the Jewish people ever rejected was Jesus. So, that means that Jesus is now the head of the Jewish faith. But, that can't be right because the rabbis would have told me.'* At that time, I dismissed the thought. However, I always remembered it.

* * * * *

The time had come to take the test. Everything rested on the final exam, including my graduation,

> I came to one of the Psalms, which says, "The stone that the builders rejected has become the chief cornerstone." I thought to myself, 'Who was rejected by the fathers of the faith?'

and therefore, my future. I hadn't been to a lecture since the second week. I was walking up the hill to class, but I was growing increasingly anxious. At that precise moment, I had the flashback.

I recalled the moment when I was 12 and the precise thought I had when I was reading that Hallel Psalm. As I paced up the hill to take the exam, out of nowhere, another thought occurred to me—*'Maybe Jesus is the head of the faith.'*

It was very strange. It just occurred to me. But, I was desperate. I needed help. I believed I was not going to graduate. *'This will be very embarrassing, and humiliating.'* I didn't know what to do. Then I suddenly burst out loud, *"Oh, Jesus help me!"*

Here I was, a Jewish guy all the way. I had a Bar Mitzvah and five years of Hebrew school. Now I was making this spontaneous appeal based on a passing thought from when I was 12 years old.

4—"Jesus, Help me!"

I continued the walk to the exam room. I decided ahead of time that no matter what was on the test, I was going to answer with what I heard during the first two weeks of class. I felt I understood the professor's basic philosophy from that first two weeks. At least, I hoped I did. That was my strategy and I went with it. That was what I put down on my final exam, regardless of the question.

They were all essay questions. When the grades were released, I had an A on the test. However I got a B+ in the course even though that exam was the only grade. I decided that was the ding because I hadn't been to class. Apparently, the professor *had* noticed I was not there for his lectures. I never did figure out how I got an A on the final when nothing else counted, but received a B+ for the course. I was certainly not complaining.

I knew something really unusual had happened to me. Why did that idea come into my mind—to say, *"Jesus, help me!"*? However, once I got what I wanted, I didn't give it another thought. I chalked it up to coincidence and it was gone. It may have been something. Maybe it was. Maybe it wasn't.

Economics provided me with a liberal arts diploma, so I graduated college. Today, Economics is a very desirable degree. However, at that time, it was not highly valued. Business considered it more art than science. But, I did graduate from college, which meant I now had a future beyond driving a truck. I believed the prevailing wisdom—*if you have a college degree, you can get a job*. At one time, it was true. It was true in my parent's generation. But, in my generation, it was no longer the case.

5—Practical Susan

During my third semester at the University of Wisconsin (UW), my roommate and I decided to have a get-together at our apartment. At UW, the drinking age was 18. A mutual friend fixed me up with Susan Dulsky, for this party.

Susan was a year and a half younger than me. In September of 1961, she was just beginning UW. After the party, I walked her home. She revealed that her father died when she was ten, and that her widowed mother raised her. During that first few weeks of school, she acknowledged she was overwhelmed. She really didn't have a father figure in her life, so she began to ask me for advice, and I started to coach her.

That was the beginning of the association. For Susan, I became a ready resource of information on how to navigate university life. She thought I was clever. She listened to what I had to say, and things seemed to work out for her. But, it was still a bit of a tumultuous relationship.

My routine was to go out with girls a maximum of three times, and then ditch them. Only a few girls would I date five times. On my second date with Susan, we were sitting in the balcony of a movie theater. I reached over to kiss her on the neck. Quite loudly, she blurted out, *"What do you think you're doing!"* The way she said it, the entire theater could hear her. That led to a colossal fight. We didn't go out again for two or three months.

After that, I needed a companion for another party, so I asked Susan, and she was okay with it. Then we would have another fight, and we wouldn't talk for a few months. This went off and on for a couple of years. I dated a lot of other girls and she dated a lot of other guys. That was typical in the 60s.

Susan was also not a great student. In fact, she was flunking out. I was vaguely aware of this. She called me for advice, and I gave it to her. Then, another couple of months passed when we didn't see one another.

One day, I was home for summer vacation when I got a telephone call. It was Susan Dulsky. I assumed she wanted to borrow some money. Why else would she be calling? Girls didn't typically call guys. *"Oh yeah. Hi, Susan. How are you? Gee, it's unusual for you to call. I guess you're probably calling because you want to borrow some money? Is that it?"*

I figured since her mother was a widow and she didn't have much money, that was the purpose for the call. *"No! Why would you think that?"* She had merely decided, *'If I don't call this guy, I'm never going to hear from him again.'*

Then she said, *"Why don't you come over? I haven't seen you in a while."*

So, I headed over to her place. After I arrived, we were sitting around her mother's apartment, visiting, when I said, *"Come September, you're going back to school. You will have to declare a major."*

She hesitated, *"That's the thing, Paul. I'm not going back. I flunked out."*

"Are you sure?"

"Yes. I appealed it and everything. I'm not going to be returning to college."

I thought for a moment. *"You know, maybe this is still solvable."*

She wasn't so sure. *"It sounds impossible to me."*

"Susan, I have an idea."

Now I had her interest. *"What's your idea?"*

"Why don't you go to the board of deans and explain that your father passed away? Don't tell them you were ten years old

when he passed away. Just tell them, 'My father passed away, and I was very upset. That's why I flunked out. It was a terrible experience, but I think I'm over it now. If you give me one more chance, I believe I'll be okay. But I need this one more opportunity.'"

Susan had nothing to lose, so she went to the board with my cockamamie story. It worked! She was allowed back into college.

I explained to her that was just the beginning of her solution. She needed a plan to do better. She was attempting to be a nurse administrator. That called for a lot of heavy-duty science courses that she couldn't get past.

When I graduated, Susan was in her junior year. I told her: *"You've attended the University of Wisconsin for a couple of years. It would be cheaper if you enrolled in a smaller school in Chicago such as Roosevelt University. You've always been good at languages. Why don't you get out of this nursing thing? You're never going to graduate. You are having chronic difficulties with all these science courses.*

"Why don't you become a language major? Get your mother a degree. She's invested all this money in your education. Your mother is working three jobs to put you through college."

At the same time as I was advocating this plan, I was aware I was coming under an obligation of sorts. I knew, according to my proposal, we were both going to be in Chicago together. I was the one that recommended she move. She was also aware of it.

However, the plan made sense, so Susan acted on it. She moved to Chicago and changed schools *and* her major. What I recommended, worked. She made all A's and B's in her new major–Spanish–and she received her degree in Languages.

Things were getting more serious for us. Now, we were dating, and I was aware that circumstances were closing in on me. Finally, at some point, I made a decision. *'I need to get out of this.'*

5—Practical Susan

It wasn't Susan. I was always genuinely afraid of *commitment*. That was the reason I only dated girls two or three times and no more. I did *not* want the *commitment*. For that reason, I became very uncomfortable with the direction things were heading between us.

Ultimately, I went over to her apartment and asked her to come downstairs. We sat in the car and I started in, *"Listen Susan, we're breaking up."*

To which she responded, *"I'm not going to let you go."*

"Susan, don't you understand? I'm not going to call you anymore."

"I'm not going to let you go."

I was firm. *"If you write me, it'll come back 'Return to Sender.'"*

She was steadfast. *"I'm not going to let you go."*

I was frustrated. *"This is a ridiculous conversation. You don't have the say-so. Do you understand? You're never going to see me again. This is it. I have to do this. It'll be better for you."*

Same response. *"I'm not going to let you go."*

It went back and forth and back and forth, and her answer was the same. *"I'm not going to let you go."*

In the end, I took Susan back upstairs to her apartment and left. That was that, and I went home. All the way to my place, I was thinking, *'What does she mean, she's not going to let me go? What does that mean exactly?'*

Once I arrived at my house, I began to pace the floor. I was really stirred up by this ridiculous conversation. I thought I was going to have a completed transaction. I was a free man. But no, she's not going to let me go! *'What am I going to do? She's not going to let me go! What does that even mean?'*

What she was saying was, *"It's not over until it's over for both of us."* What was I going to do? I couldn't bring myself to hurt her. That, I couldn't do. If she would have said *"Okay,"* I would have been fine with it. That would have been it because, if it was okay with her, it was okay with me. But, she wouldn't have any of it.

Then, I began to think, *'You know, if she is not going to let me go, that means eventually we're going to get married . . . Paul, if you're going to do it eventually, you better take the plunge and get it over with, because you don't want to spend years and years anguishing over this.'*

It was 1964. I was 22, and the Vietnam War was starting to heat up. The draft was becoming a big thing in 1964. I could see that the Viet Nam War was going to get bigger—*maybe a lot bigger! 'If I do it now, I'll be a married man. I won't be such an obvious candidate for the draft.'*

I did not feel that the United States was in any real danger. I was not an anti-war demonstrator. I just never felt the country was in any danger. I didn't see our country as vulnerable in the slightest way. That was my opinion. That was the reason why I did not want to be drafted.

In the end, I took a page from the playbook of my grandfather, Bernard Liberman, and my father, Marvin Liberman. My grandfather was married in 1917, and my father was born in 1918. My grandfather was a World War I eligible draftee, yet my grandfather slipped through. My mother's father, Herman Screiber, also conveniently married in 1917 and avoided the draft.

My father was married in 1940. He missed out on the draft in WWII when I was born in January, 1942. I believed it was fine to slip through myself, by all legal means. I still considered myself very much an establishment guy, but that was my sentiment on the war.

I was pacing back and forth in my apartment with all of these thoughts. *'If you're going to take the plunge, just do it!'* The next day, I went downtown and bought a diamond ring.

What I did next, I meant to be humorous—an ice breaker. I took the ring out of the jeweler's box and put it into a plain brown paper sack. Susan was making lunch, and I was eating a hot dog. Then I handed her the paper bag. The sack had the ring in it, but nothing else. She opened the bag and had a puzzled look on her face. *"There's nothing in it?"* She didn't see the ring.

I urged her to take another look. *"It's not empty. Look again. It's in there."*

Just the day before, she had said she was not going to let me go! Now, she saw the ring and she just went airborne. She was so thrilled *and* she saw the humor in it. *'We were going to do this differently. We were going to have a story.'*

Eventually, she calmed down. Then she said, *"Paul, this is wonderful. Of course I want to marry you, but you need to take the ring back."*

> I was pacing back and forth in my apartment with all of these thoughts. *'If you're going to take the plunge, just do it!'*

I was really confused. *"Why?"*

Without missing a beat, she responded, *"We're going to need the money."* The ring had cost me $600, and she was unwavering that we could use that $600 to get started. Practical Susan.

I insisted she keep the ring. I was adamant. *"No! We'll make the money, but you should have a ring."*

When Susan realized I was steadfast, she relented. *"Okay, we can save on other things, because we're going to need money to get started. Let's just have a private ceremony. We can go down to the court and only have our parents and family there. Or, maybe we can have it in some rabbi's private study."*

I was resolute. *"No, this is a once in a lifetime deal. A girl should have a wedding, so we're going to have the wedding."*

Later, she would raise the same objection to having a honeymoon. *"We can use the money to get started."*

Now it was time to plan for the wedding. My parents, her mother, and Susan and I were all sitting around the dining room table organizing the wedding. They were all talking at the same time. One said to call the florist, and another said to do something else. We need this list and this and that item. A long discussion ensued about where we were going to have the wedding.

I was sitting there and wasn't saying a word. As all this "planning" was taking place, I was slowly sinking into my chair. I was getting more and more panicky about the entire thing. The reality was starting to sink in. I always had a fear of commitment, and this anxiety was raising its head.

I didn't believe I could make it long term as a husband. It was just too much of an obligation—too much commitment, too much baggage, too much responsibility. I just couldn't see myself doing that. I was sure it wasn't for me. But, if it wasn't Susan, it would be nobody. I was sure of that much.

In the end, I concluded I was going to do it. I did not want to hurt Susan. After about two hours of listening to the conversation all around me, I finally spoke up. *"Listen. You all need to understand this has to happen within 60 days or I can't make it. I'll be calling the whole thing off. I won't be able to make it through. But, if you make it within 60 days, I'll try my best to make it happen."*

Nobody said a word. Nobody debated with me. They all knew I was petrified. Everything turned on a dime. *"You do this ...You do that."* Nobody cared what anybody else did. There was no time for hurt feelings. Just get it done!

It all got done in a rush, and it all worked smoothly. Everyone was appreciative that each person was doing their part. Susan and I were married August 22, 1964, which also happened to be her 21st birthday.

After the ceremony, we were at the airport about to leave for our honeymoon in Miami. Susan said she wanted to call her mother. She asked me, *"Can you give me a dime?"* That was the cost of a phone call in 1964.

I was shocked. *"You don't have a dime?*

"I don't even have a dime." We always made a joke of it. When Susan came into the marriage, she had no money. She didn't even have a dime!

We left on our honeymoon to Miami. We stayed in one of the high-rise hotels, the Eden Roc, near the top floor. All of a sudden, we heard someone pounding at our door. We figured it was kids playing around, so we just didn't answer. We didn't want to be bothered. As it turned out, there was a hurricane about to hit landfall. It was hurricane season in South Florida!

In the morning, we woke up and most of the hotel windows were broken. The lobby was completely flooded. We went through the entire Hurricane Cleo, absolutely oblivious—a category two hurricane with winds over 100 mph! What a way to start a marriage!

6—Deal Maker

After I graduated from college, I went back to work in the family's electrical supply business. With a liberal arts degree, where are you going to go? I worked in the shipping room, I made deliveries, and I worked at the sales counter. I even went out and did sales. I was 22 years old, and I knew the business.

But I was only making $6,000 a year. And, I was trying to support a wife and start a family. That was not a lot of money. Before we were married, to make it formal with her mother, I asked her for Susan's hand in marriage. I had only recently received a raise to $6,600 a year.

"Paul, can you support her? Do you make enough working in the electrical business?"

That was a good question. In 1964, $6,600 a year was okay, but it left nothing extra. I was always a long-range planner of sorts. Now that I was working in the family business, I began thinking, *'How is this going to work in the long run? I don't have a marketable degree. This electrical business is not real good. I have three brothers, and my father owns 50% of the business. That means, I'm going to have a whopping 12.5% of a not very successful company! My father is a young man, and when my father passes away, this is what I have to look forward to inheriting.'*

About this time, I saw the company books for the first time. I immediately became aware that for the previous eleven years the business had *lost* money. It was a shocking revelation.

That's when it began to dawn on me, *'I'm really trapped! Where am I going? What else am I going to do? This is the business I know. Nobody else is going to hire me in the industry. They'd be certain I was a spy for another company, the Libermans. This is the only field I know. I'm really stuck.'* I started to realize I had really painted myself into a corner by squandering my educational opportunity on a non-marketable degree.

Unexpectedly, something happened to change the equation. Not long after I graduated from college, the company purchasing agent—the guy who did the wholesale buying for the business— left for another job. That created a big hole to fill.

'I'm really trapped! Where am I going? What else am I going to do?'

There were very few positions in the company. My father was confident I knew the business. Who else was there? He always believed I was a very capable guy. He was a very good administrator; however, he was not a risk taker. He always had a lot of valuable common sense, but he was not an entrepreneur.

I was 22 years old when my father made the decision to install me into the recently vacated buyer's position. He always had a great deal of confidence in me and he told everyone, *"Paul can do this."*

I began to consider the situation. *'Maybe there are possibilities here. If I do a good job, we can do a lot of sales. If you buy something right, it's half sold. I'll sharpen my pencil. I'll buy right, and we will sell right. I can do something with this job.'*

I learned everything about being a buyer. I started making deals. My father knew I was a risk taker. I know he started to wonder, *'Is Paul going to take too much risk?'* He was averse to risk. He was a straightforward businessman.

I began to consider, *'How do I make more money? We have to make this operation bigger! How do I make it bigger?'* My solution was to start making deals. Then things really begin to click and we were making money. I became the dealmaker for the business. All the salesmen knew, *"Paul's the dealmaker. The old man runs the business, but Paul's the dealmaker."*

After a while, my father was okay with this. *"Paul, just go to it!"* He didn't even want to know the details. Whatever I was doing, *"Just do it."* It was working.

I was now a 23-year-old wheeler-dealer. In fact, I was negotiating deals beyond what the company could afford. But, we were making money. Based on the revenue we were now taking in, my father was able to go to the bank and borrow more. He was fine with that, because Paul was making profitable deals. Business was lucrative for the first time in a long time. The company was turning around.

I started working in 1964, after my graduation from college. By 1967, we were wheeling and dealing and the company was becoming successful. Personally, I was still struggling financially. The company was giving me small raises, but at least they were giving me raises. By that time, I was making $7,775 annually–nothing great.

In 1966, Susan and I were having our first child and I was convinced I had to make more money. The neighborhood where we lived was changing; it was getting dangerous. We lived on a boulevard. It was difficult to push a baby buggy down a busy thoroughfare. We knew it was time to buy a house.

We had $1,100 in the bank. It was clear to me, *'I've got to do it because prices are going up.'* So, in February, 1967, with only a $7,800 annual salary, I plunked my money down on a house, to be constructed in a development. I gave my $1,100 to the builder as the down payment. This was all we had managed to save during our first three years of marriage.

I heard it was possible to obtain a home loan with 5% to 10% down. I was counting on that. With that understanding, I signed the contract. I told the builder, *"It's okay with me if it takes longer to build our house. The longer it takes, the more time I have to make and save money."*

It eventually took 10 months to construct the house. The important thing was that the price was locked in. During the ten months, I was constantly wondering, *'How am I going to make more money?'* There was just so much money I could get from my salary. In the business things were improving, but the small raises I received had yet to meet my expectations.

Then, I received a jolt from the contractor's home loan representative. *"No, Mr. Liberman. We actually require a 20% down payment."*

I had already delivered all my savings to the builder and now I find out that PMI–Private Mortgage Insurance–which made it possible to obtain a 90%–95% loan, was *not* available through the builder I contracted with! They really *did* require 20% down! *'Where am I going to get this money?'*

I had written a check for $1,100 when we signed the contract. I had ten months to save, and otherwise come up with an additional $5,500. *'Even 10% was going to be tough. How am I going to do it?'*

That's when I began to ask for builder credits. *"Instead of oak wood floors, can I have plywood? We don't even need a carpet."* I started making subtractions. *"Don't do this. Work with me. Give me a credit against my down payment."*

The price was fixed at $33,000. Builder's credits were applied as credits toward my down payment. I was struggling to make the 20% down payment on a $33,000 home–*$6,600. 'Where am I going to get the difference?'*

"I don't need this, I don't need that." The creative system of builder's credits helped bridge the gap but I was still substantially short.

At that point, I made a decision. *'I'm going to sell my blood.'*

I went down to Michael Reese Hospital. I was in the waiting area with all the drunks who were *also* selling their blood. I discovered you could only sell blood once every two months. I was prodding the staff to let me sell *more* blood. I was pushing the time limit.

I didn't exactly look like their "regulars." The hospital staff wanted to know why I was so desperate to sell my blood, so I explained the situation. Eventually, the woman at the desk clued me in, *"We have an experimental program where you can sell your blood more frequently. We*

> I discovered you could only sell blood once every two months.

take a pint of your blood and we swirl it in a centrifuge. We take out the red corpuscles, and we give you back the white. Then we take another pint. But you can't do this more than twice a week."

That sounded great to me! For ten months, that's exactly what I did. I went to Michael Reese Hospital twice a week to sell my plasma for the experimental program. That was good for about $1,000. One side effect of removing the red corpuscles was that it made me very tired. All the iron was gone. But, I discovered, within 72 hours my blood would replace the iron.

I still needed more money. At that juncture, I came up with another plan. I decided I would go into the credit-card business. I had always paid my bills, so I was able to obtain an account at a number of the major department stores. They each had their own store credit card. At the time, MasterCard and Visa were just getting started.

I went into the stores where I had a credit account and bought a gift certificate for $100 on my card. Afterward, I would buy a bag of peanuts with the certificate and get the change in cash. Now I owed $100 on my bill, but I had $97 in cash. Then I bought another $100 gift certificate, and so on.

I went around to all the department stores borrowing money this way. Between the blood business, the credit card business, and the builder's credits, I squeaked into the closing and we owned our house.

Now it was time to move our furniture from the apartment to the new house. I rented a truck and recruited all my friends to help move the furniture. It would have been unthinkable to pay for a mover. After we relocated the furniture and paid for the truck, I had $5 cash left over. For $5, I bought every one of my "assistants" hamburgers, and Susan and I were in the house.

Of course, there were slivers in the floor from the plywood, but we were in the house and we owned it. In the meantime, I was plugging along, making the mortgage payments, and endeavoring to build up the business; but we were barely making it. We had an old, used car.

On the bright side, I was really grateful I had been able to lock in the price one year before we took possession. The house continued to appreciate in value. As I had figured, prices were rising. Over the next three years, the $33,000 house appreciated in value by $15,000—almost 50%.

I was working in the business as hard as I could, making deals. And, things were constantly improving. I was already starting to pay attention to the commodity markets. I began to focus on commodities in another effort to make more money for the business. My eyes were wide open as to how they worked— very high leverage with potentially wild price swings.

One of my routine purchases for the company was copper wire, a staple in the electrical industry. One day, I recognized a definite trend—the price of copper was steadily rising. I promptly made the decision the business should buy a lot of copper wire, as much as possible.

Since the business had always paid its bills, I could order and our suppliers would deliver. I promptly purchased $600,000 worth of copper wire, which would be valued at millions of dollars today.

I was gambling the future of the company that the price of copper would continue to rise.

Immediately, I took off for a three-week vacation. Susan and I drove out west where no one could find me. We were on our trip. Intentionally, no one could find me. It was 1966, and Susan was pregnant with Joel, our first child.

> **I was gambling the future of the company that the price of copper would continue to rise.**

The wire was being delivered, but by design, they couldn't locate me. (Obviously, this was before cell phones.) Truckloads of copper wire were constantly arriving in our warehouse. I know what I'm doing, but nobody else knows. Everyone just sees these truckloads of wire being delivered. They certainly aren't aware how *much* I ordered. In addition to our regular purchases, I did additional *super* purchases.

Prices were rising quickly—mostly because of the Viet Nam War. I was correct about the upward trends. Eventually, I returned from vacation. Right away, I received a call from one of several wire company suppliers. (I purchased from more than one company.)

It was our main supplier. *"Paul, you've got these very large orders here. Are you prepared to take delivery? Do you have the warehouse space to take all this stuff? We're about ready to ship it to you. Do you want to cancel any of these orders?"*

I knew it was a bluff. There were such shortages *they* couldn't get all the wire they needed. I knew that. *"No, no. Bring it on. We're ready. We've got the warehouse space. We're expecting you."*

Had I *not* had enough storage space, I was prepared to rent another warehouse. I was determined we would be ready. *"Bring the wire! I'll hire some men to do the unloading. Should we expect it this afternoon or tomorrow?"* I called their bluff. And, the copper wire was delivered. We were a major client.

The price of copper wire more than doubled. It increased from $6.56 a foot to $14.79. And, I had all the sizes of wire. I was correct. Afterward, I started making transactions with our customers. *"I bought it at a great price and I can give you some. How much can you use?"* We quickly sold everything. We were able to undercut all of our competition because we bought at the right price. The business was now making money hand over fist. That year we made $300,000 in profit.

Before I became the buyer, the company had been losing money. With my deal making, we were now in the black. It was a super year because of the copper wire contracts I had negotiated. Not only did we become a profitable business, but we had become a *very* lucrative company.

When it became clear how much we had made, my father came to me to complain. *"Paul, we're going to have a boatload of taxes to pay."* He was already preparing me not to expect such a large bonus. He and my Uncle Harold were taking $30,000 to $50,000 in bonuses as a result of the profits I had generated. For the two of them, it was hallelujah time after years of scarcity and hard work.

'At last, our ship has come in!'

My father was complaining to me about the taxes because he was aware I knew we were making a bundle of money. His strategy was to avoid paying this youngster in his 20s a chunk of money such as he and Uncle Harold were receiving.

I knew immediately what was going on. Almost instantly, I had an inspirational idea how to solve the tax problem. *"A boatload of taxes? You know Dad, I might have an idea about how we can beat that. We have a competitor that has also been losing money for a very long time. I happen to know they've been losing money for 14 years.* " It was a declining industry.

"We could buy them out. Their tax loss carry forwards would offset all our profits and then some!"

My father looked confused *"Is that right? Are you sure?"*

"Why not? It all makes sense to me."

He wasn't so sure. *"I'll have to see it in writing."*

In short order, I made an appointment to see my old school chum. We had grown up together. He was now a lawyer and an accountant. I explained the situation and told him about my proposed solution. We headed to the law library. In the regulations, he showed me that my idea was correct. I made copies of the specific paragraphs that applied and brought them to my father.

He couldn't believe it. *"It looks right, but I'm not sure I trust your friend. The IRS is serious business."*

"Dad, just call your accountant, who works in the same office with your lawyer. Read all of this to them or show it to them. They'll confirm this is correct."

My father showed all of this to his accountant, and he conferred with the lawyer who was in the same office.

"It really wouldn't apply to your circumstance." They gave some vague and muddled reason for their opinion. I was certain they didn't *want* it to be true! This youngster came up with a solution and they hadn't. My father told me what they said. *"For this particular situation it wouldn't work."*

"Look, Dad, I'm sure it's on point. Your lawyer and your accountant don't know what the heck they're talking about." It was 1967 and I was only 25 years old, but my father had a lot of confidence in me. He wanted to believe me. *"What am I supposed to do? Listen to you or listen to my accountant and my attorney?"*

I wasn't letting this go. *"I have a solution. We need to ask Arthur Anderson—worldwide accountants—for a letter of opinion. Find out one way or the other who is right. I am that certain."*

"Paul, that's going to be expensive."

I had already checked on the price of an opinion letter. *"It will cost you $2,000. Look at all the money you can save for $2,000!"* At that time, tax rates were close to 70%.

He agreed, and Arthur Anderson wrote the letter. It confirmed everything I said. I was proven correct, and my father's accountant and attorney were wrong. After the buyout of the other company, our business had so many losses to carry forward that the transaction not only helped us offset profits for that year but for several future years.

It was a bonanza between the wire purchases and the tax loss carry forwards. Things were really great. Paul—the young punk who was the dealmaker of the business—had done it. Now, my father believed I was the cat's meow.

Bonus time came, and my father and Uncle Harold were taking their hefty bonuses—$30,000–$40,000. I am waiting for mine. Now is the big payoff–the big one! I can only imagine. Everything I've been working for has come to this!

I fumbled to get the envelope open. There it was–a $500 bonus check. All that work. I was devastated. In their minds, I was this 25-year-old kid. *"What should he expect?"*

7—"Jesus, Help Me, *Again*!"

It was December 1967. The end of the year was around the corner, and the business had a *great* year—the best year in the company's history. I was aware the two owners—Uncle Harold and my father, Marvin Liberman—were taking large bonuses. I was expecting to pick up maybe $10,000, or $5,000 *at a minimum*.

When I did receive my end-of-the-year bonus check on December 31, 1967, *it was $500*. I was 25 and totally demoralized. Everyone was aware I generated the revenue that turned the company around. I had come up with the solution to completely cover the taxes on the business profits. The partners were raking in the bucks for the first time in a decade, and loving it. They were also oblivious to my despondency.

I was always in awe of my father. I would never overtly challenge him. Even as a small boy, I was intimidated by him. I never knew where I stood. I never felt I had his general approval. In business, I had his respect. Other than that, I didn't feel he was interested in me. I wanted him to know me better, and I wanted to know him better. But, he was not the kind of man who could relate to *anyone* on a sentimental basis. When I was younger, that filled me with a bit of rebellion. As an adult, I felt emotionally shortchanged by him.

Somewhat timidly, I attempted to discuss the bonus matter with my father. He was obviously uncomfortable with the conversation. He indicated it was out of his hands and implied his brother had made the decision.

I began to hope, perhaps they would make it up in salary. For the balance of the year, I waited for the anticipated pay raise. When I did receive one, it was 15¢ an hour—a token. I crossed the $8,000 threshold for annual income. *'Big deal.'*

After the 15¢ raise, it hit me. *'Paul, this is always how it's going to be. You're going to be the slave—forever. That's the way they see you.'*

I felt very much betrayed—very disappointed. What was worse, I had no hope. I could imagine nothing that would break the cycle. I was profoundly troubled. I was in a real muddle because I pictured the rest of my life going the same way—barely treading water.

The more I pondered it, the more convinced I became there was no exit. One night, I came home and opened up to Susan. *"I'm really in a funk about all this. I can't shake it. I don't know what else to do. I've got to get away and figure out what to do about life in general. I don't see any change ever coming over the horizon. My father and Uncle Harold are never going to share the profits with me. I will always be the little red hen that makes the deals. I'm the young guy, I'm the kid. I have to get away and figure this out."*

Susan knew this was serious. *"Where are you going to go?"*

"It's the winter. I'm heading down to Florida. I'm going alone to Miami."

I packed a few things and left. I stayed with my grandparents, but I was only sleeping there. I did not wish to discuss anything with them, otherwise it would be transmitted instantly to Chicago.

> The more I pondered it, the more convinced I became there was no exit.

I couldn't shake the situation. Mostly, I walked the streets. One night, I decided to go to the movies to see *Camelot.* Afterward, I walked out of the theater and directly to my car. I was really struck with the idea of doing something significant with my life. However, I saw no chance of it.

7—"Jesus, Help me, *Again!*"

There was no way up for me in the family business. I didn't have a real education. I had no real options. Now I had a wife and children and a mortgage. I had plenty of debt. I could see no way out of this trick bag. *'I have to find a way to do something significant and meaningful. Otherwise, I'm just going to tread water for the rest of my life.'*

I was distraught. Then I began to weep and sob. I was emotional after the movie, and now I was crying uncontrollably. Once again, I had become a desperate man. At that moment, I recalled my college experience when I had been in nearly as hopeless a place. That was also an impossible situation—a single exam standing between me and graduation.

I remembered the entire episode with the course final and how that turned out. *'Why not? What do I have to lose?'*

'I have to find a way to do something significant and meaningful. Otherwise, I'm just going to tread water for the rest of my life.'

With that thought, sitting there in my car in the dark, I began to call out loud. *"Oh, Jesus, help me! You've got to find a way out for me. I can't do this any longer. Oh, Jesus, please help me!"* That's all I knew to say. I didn't know anything else *to* say. It was the most desperate thing I could reach for.

8—Precinct Worker

I headed back to Chicago after my visit to Miami. Nothing had changed, but I felt a little better because I had been away for a week. Not long after I returned, Susan and I were sitting around the house visiting when I abruptly stopped and stared at Susan.

"There's something wrong with my Grandfather Bernard in Florida."

"Paul, what do you mean?"

"There's something wrong with his pacemaker."

"Nah, that can't be. Those things last at least four years, and he's only had his four months!"

"No, there's something wrong with it. I'm certain."

"There's one way to find out. Give him a call."

I immediately placed a call to Miami and what I said was correct. My grandfather was in the hospital in intensive care. It was very serious. I had described his circumstance exactly. I was really puzzled by the way this happened. How could I, while sitting on a couch in Chicago, know what was happening with my grandfather in Miami?

A few days later, I was talking with one of the industry salesmen at work. We were kind of pals, so I told him how, out of the blue, I had known about what was happening with my grandfather. He began to relate to me information concerning a lady he said could do this sort of thing with regularity.

"She lives in your neighborhood. She does this all the time. You can find out from her what is going on. Just ask her."

At my first opportunity, I looked her up and went to see her. I told her all about what happened with my Grandfather. In response to my story, she began to make a number of predictions about me—predictions which did eventually come true.

8—Precinct Worker

"Something this year is going to result in something next year and will result in your making a long business trip to the east. You will be moving east. You will be in your new house by Christmas." Then, she invited me to a group meeting coming up.

When I arrived at the get-together, everyone was standing in a circle praying to Jesus. This freaked me out. I snuck away at the first opportunity, absolutely determined not to see her again. The psychic part I liked. It was the Jesus part I could not handle. But, she had already made her predictions. *I would be relocating. I would make a long distance move to the East. I would be in my new house by Christmas.* What she said was very specific.

After my abrupt trip to Florida, I began to feel better, although I was still thinking a lot about my predicament. I was marooned in a job and a company with no conceivable upside. Then, an idea began to occur to me. It was 1968—a major election year.

I began to consider that politics might be my way out of the trick bag—the occupational trap I was caught in. In politics, education isn't the major issue. All anyone considers is your competence.

I wasn't thinking about going to work for the government. I planned to work as a volunteer for Republican candidates and, in the process, to prove my value. The elections were about to get underway, and there were many candidates who required volunteers.

I would demonstrate to them that I was quite competent. Perhaps I could extract myself, in this way, from the Liberman family business trap. My objective was to do an end-run around my entire family electrical-business dilemma. By establishing personal competence, other doors would potentially open.

I was a Goldwater Republican. I went to the local township, but it was not so easy to get started. *"We don't have anything for you. Maybe you can assist our precinct captain."* I put flyers under the windshield wipers. I went door to door. I walked the precinct.

Anything I was asked, because it needed to be done. Sure enough, it all congealed in 1969. When the precinct captain moved on, I became the new precinct captain.

There was an Illinois constitutional convention coming up. I made the decision to study up on the state constitution. I was 26 years old and did not lack confidence. *'Surely I must know a lot about the Constitution of Illinois!'* Afterward, I wrote a 43-page paper detailing what steps should be taken to modify the Constitution.

> **I put flyers under the windshield wipers. I went door to door. I walked the precinct.**

Eventually, there was a steering committee meeting of the nominating committee. I took my 43-page paper and attended. There were eleven contenders seeking to be the delegate from our township—the suburbs of south Chicago. I did *not* get slated. I didn't realize it, but the fix was in. It was obvious. I had done my homework on the topic of the Constitution. I was prepared. I knew the subject. The man selected as the delegate, did not. I was greatly disappointed.

A short time later, I had lunch with a Republican friend of mine. I told him what happened and how disappointed I was after writing the 43-page paper. *"Paul, they see what they did to you. All is not lost. Be smart. Donate $200 to the candidate—the guy you lost to. It will be the largest contribution for his campaign, which is extraordinary. Nobody is going to take an interest in this. If you donate $200, you'll be the big donor."*

I followed his advice. I contributed $200, which was scarce money on my budget. As a result, I became the campaign manager.

It wasn't just a two party race. There were an abundance of potential applicants from other Illinois districts. There were plenty of people who wanted to have a hand in rewriting the Illinois

Constitution. As campaign manager, this was an opportunity to show my stuff.

I worked very hard and developed a complete team of people to help me. I really organized. I had plenty of volunteers out working. When it was over, we swamped every other candidate— by 10 to 1! Now everybody knew me. *"You know, Paul is a competent fellow. Look at that."*

9—Slated

Our district had an opening for the Illinois State Legislature. A couple of my political buddies put a bug in my ear. *"Paul, why don't you go before the nominating committee? We think you'll have a shot at becoming the candidate."*

My reputation was growing. I was very active in all the different aspects of Republican Party affairs in the township. Everyone knew me. I had been working long hours as a campaign volunteer for almost a year. Sure enough, at 27 years old, I was slated as the Republican candidate for the Illinois legislature. In my particular district, if you were the Republican candidate, you were certain of a victory. I began to assemble my campaign team. After that, news of my nomination hit the local newspapers. I could see my exit ticket: *'I'm getting out of the electrical business! I was right! I had a good theory and it worked!'*

That's when I received a phone call.

"Congratulations Mr. Liberman. We understand you are the slated candidate for the district. There are three of us who wish to have lunch with you." My curiosity was peaked. I readily agreed and a lunch was arranged.

"Paul, the reason we wanted to see you is that we own land in your district. In fact, we've been acquiring a lot of land. We believe there needs to be a third major airport in Chicago. We believe that airport should be on the south side, in your district. We have a plan and we want you to carry the ball for us in the state legislature."

They proceeded to lay out their development plans at

> **We believe there needs to be a third major airport in Chicago. We believe that airport should be on the south side, in your district.**

the lunch table. At the same time as they were presenting it, they were closely observing my reaction.

I tried to sound enthusiastic. *"It looks good to me. I can do that. Of course there are probably other people that have plans for this airport."*

"Yes Paul, there are. And we need to know you are going to back our plan."

Now, I was feeling a bit uncomfortable. I hesitated. *"What are you saying? I think I can, but I'm sure you would agree I owe it to the public, and to myself, to consider all the other plans as well."*

"That won't be good enough Mr. Liberman. Before we get up from this table, you are going to commit to advocating our plan, or you're not. You have to give us an answer before we leave this table."

The easiest thing would have been to go along. That is what they were expecting. *'Sure thing guys. I'm your man.'*

However, there was a coercive element in this entire get-together which didn't sit right with me. I was the candidate. I was in solid. I was also young and naïve, so I informed them, *"I will do my best for you, but I can't commit without first gathering all the facts, including hearing any alternative proposals."* I didn't appreciate the intimidating aspect of their tone.

Almost immediately after the lunch, these men made a decision to unseat me. This led me to do some investigation. I discovered there was Mafia money behind these guys, although I had no clue when I met with them. They were buying up land in the district, and people in the township knew it and knew their intentions. These guys had arranged the luncheon appointment with me. The assumption was, *'We have this idealistic young man, Paul Liberman, right? We'll put him out there as the face of our project. He'll do what we need him to do.'*

10—The Kingmaker

I was slated as the Republican candidate in a safe Republican district. Due to my youthful inexperience, I had antagonized a handful of constituents who had "questionable" business connections.

Now, they were determined to unseat and replace me as the candidate, even though my selection had already been made public by the media.

I was searching for a solution to this pickle. That led me to call on the most senior party man I knew in the township. He happened to work for *Standard Oil of Indiana*. I detailed the entire lunch meeting I had with the "businessmen" and related the plans the men had for the proposed Chicago airport. I also told him what my investigation had uncovered regarding their "community ties." *"What should I do? Now they're attempting to pull strings and have me replaced as the candidate."*

"Paul, I really don't know. You're now in the big leagues. I actually don't know what to advise you, but I do know who would be able to. Let me give him a call and then get back to you."

In a little while, as promised, I received a callback. *"Paul, are you available for breakfast on Tuesday?"* Without hesitation, I agreed. At the scheduled breakfast, I met Charlie Barr for the first time, a man who would change my life. Charlie worked as an assistant to the Chairman of Standard Oil of Indiana. His official title was Vice-President in charge of Public Relations.

"Paul, I know all about you. I've been following your career. I saw what you did with the constitutional convention matter. Now I see that you're slated for the Illinois legislature."

He knew all about my predicament.

"If you fight them, you'll still win your seat. But, you will have to fight them every two years. They will never quit until they unseat

you. You will never really enjoy incumbency. My recommendation–you don't fight them. Just step aside."

I immediately realized he was the real deal. He knew what he was talking about.

"Paul, you don't belong in state politics. It's too corrupt. You belong in national politics. If you are ready for this, I can help you. If you agree, I want you to come over to my house every Saturday. I'm going to teach you the ropes. We'll get started this weekend."

I knew instantly that I could trust this man. That weekend was my first of many visits to Charlie's small farm just outside of Chicago. Beginning with that meeting, every Saturday I would show up. Over a glass of beer, he would teach me the ins and outs of national politics.

"Paul, when you first meet someone, make certain the highest ranking, most influential and important person you know introduces you. The reason is, from that time on, you will be associated with the strata of importance of the person who first introduced you."

"Never put your own money into politics. Always use other people's money. As soon as you use your own money, you'll always be counted on as the schnook we go after for a few bucks, and you won't be taken seriously in other ways. You won't have money big enough, or you shouldn't have money big enough, to make a difference." There were hundreds of these little gems of wisdom. I was drinking it all in—soaking it up like a sponge.

Ours quickly became a very close and deep personal friendship. It became apparent right away that I filled an emotional void Charlie had as a result of his lack of relationship with his own sons. For me, Charlie became a role model and a father figure, filling the void of what I was missing with my own father.

Time passed and I was getting to know Charlie better and better. Then, one day in 1969, he called me. *"Listen Paul, I've been* *thinking. I have to start getting you some credentials. On December 15, we're having a $100 a plate cocktail party for Senator Ted Stevens of Alaska. Why don't you come? I want to introduce you to some people."*

One hundred dollars was a lot of money for me, but if Charlie thought it was important, I would go. I paid my money and made a personal commitment that I would drink enough booze, and eat enough hors d'oeuvres, to get my money's worth. As the evening continued, I recognized a congressman that was present, so I approached him.

"How do you do? I'm Paul Liberman."

"Oh, you're Paul Liberman?" He said it as if he knew me. *'How's he ever heard of me?'*

I had a bit more to drink. Then, I recognized Walter Hickel, the Secretary of the Interior from Alaska, so I walked up to *him.* *"How do you do Mr. Secretary? I'm very glad to meet you. My name is Paul Liberman."*

"Oh yes, Paul Liberman. Charlie mentioned your name to me." I continued making the rounds and meeting people and it seemed to be the standard shtick. I began to wonder, *'Is this just something politicians say?'* As the evening progressed, Charlie ventured over. *"Paul, we're all going out to dinner; the Congressmen, the Senators, and me. I want you to join us."*

At the restaurant, before we entered the door of the private room arranged for this exclusive gathering, Charlie pulled me aside discreetly. *"Paul, I am*

> **"Paul, we're all going out to dinner; the Congressmen, the Senators, and me. I want you to join us."**

aware that, during the primary, you opposed the incumbent, Senator Smith. You were aligned with his challenger. Do you know that in the entire state, you were the only area that won? But you did win! If you will support the Senator in the upcoming election, your entire operation will feel free to switch over. The entire township will be released to shift their support. If you do this, Paul, you will not be sorry." By this time, I had already come to understand Charlie was a "kingmaker."

"I guarantee you will never be sorry for doing this. Will you do it?"

There was nothing to think about. If Charlie said this was the thing to do, I was on board. *"Well sure. Of course."*

"Good, that means your entire crew will work for the incumbent Senator in the upcoming election. I'm going to arrange it so that you are on the Senator's campaign staff for the south suburbs of Cook County, Chicago."

There were about 10 regions, and I headed one of them. I had an entire region to oversee. Therefore, I attended campaign meetings in Springfield, the state capitol, and in Chicago. While I worked on the campaign, I did other things as well.

I was still in the electrical business, but I had already made a decision to use politics as a springboard out of that. What were they going to do, *fire me?* When I needed to be away for the campaign, I was away. I was still fulfilling my company responsibilities, but my nights and my weekends were busy with politics. If I had to disappear, or if I needed to use the Xerox machine to make copies, I would do it. I now saw the electrical vocation as a springboard into something else.

One afternoon, while Charlie was off in Rome, Italy, raising money for various campaigns, I received a phone call from Charlie's personal secretary. She was agitated and began to tell me something about a fundraiser coming up for Senator Paul Fannin of Arizona.

"Charlie says this thing is behind, and his assistant at Standard Oil of Indiana has done nothing about it. There are only 17 days remaining until the event. We will be tremendously embarrassed. You were on the last committee. Charlie wants to know, can you take charge? Can you bail us out?"

This was music to my ears. *'Ah! They need me.'*

"Sure. I'll be happy to help."

I threw myself into the task. First, I rented a room, and that made me think about how to fill it up. *'How am I gonna get people to come to this thing?'* Then, I had a truly inspired idea. I headed to the public library to do my research. I looked for all the companies that had home offices in Chicago and branch offices in Arizona.

This was before things were computerized, and it was labor intensive. After that, I put together a list of all the companies who had home offices in Arizona and branch offices in Chicago. Then, I cross-referenced the two lists. From this information, I put together another list of all the presidents and chairmen of the boards of these companies.

That was my list. These were the people I was going to invite with personal telephone calls. Within a couple of days of receiving the call from Charlie's secretary, I had rented the hall, taken care of the hors d'oeuvres, the drinks were all set, and the invitations were mailed. After that, I spent time making calls working my telephone list.

"Hello, this is Paul Liberman. I'm the Executive Director of the Midwest Fannin for Senate Committee. The Senator would like to know if you could attend a cocktail party we're having in Chicago?" The answer was usually *"Yes."*

Then I had another brainstorm. *'If I can have other dignitaries at the meeting, it will make it more attractive for all these people to say yes.'* I immediately called the Washington, DC offices of other conservative senators. *"Hello, this is Paul Liberman, Executive Director of the Midwest Fannin for Senate Committee. . . Can you have the Senator's schedule penciled in for the evening of . . ."* and I gave them the date.

Most of the secretaries said *yes*, and so I had a handful of senators and congressmen coming—all with the conservative stripe that would draw the crowd. This was a practice widely used in the political world. To *pencil it in* means—*it is cancelable*. Like a pencil mark in the planner, *it is easy to erase*. It is a commitment that *"I'll be there if nothing else comes up."* It didn't mean they were certain to come *but it was penciled in*, which would be strong enough for me to attract a crowd. Then, I thought, *'You know, this is working.'* That's when I called Vice President Spiro Agnew's office. *"Pencil it in."* Sure enough, his secretary was agreeable.

Once I had the Vice President, I was able to really milk the fact that it was on his schedule, too. This helped insure the senators would

> *"You know, this is working."'* That's when I called Vice President Spiro Agnew's office.

actually come, which insured others would come, etc. In 17 days, I raised about $20,000 from a $100 a plate cocktail party. Most importantly, I now had my own little fundraising mechanism that worked. I continued doing this for various congressmen and senators.

11—Paul, What Do You Want?

Once I successfully organized the fundraiser for Senator Paul Fannin of Arizona, I had my niche. I was promptly enlisted to do the same thing for Republican politicians around the country. For example, I was working on a senatorial campaign staff, which meant I was part of the machinery. As a result, I was getting to know congressmen and senators from a number of states.

In September of 1970, Charlie called me in for a meeting with the Executive Director of the Illinois Republican Party. I had already learned Charlie was a person who could call the White House and immediately be put through. It was just the two of us and Charlie. At this meeting, Charlie was unusually serious. *"You are the two guys I can count on to raise money. The fact is—the Republican Party in Illinois has no money left to make payroll. I have decided, I want the two of you to form a 500 club."*

Almost at the same moment, we both blurted out the same question. *"What the heck is a 500 club?"*

> I had already learned Charlie was a person who could call the White House and immediately be put through.

"I will explain. Paul, I want you to call all these executives that you've called on previously. These are men who have attended our campaign fundraisers. You're going to call them and say, 'My name is Paul Liberman. I'm Executive Director of Governor Ogilvie's 500 Club.' They're going to ask you, 'What's the 500 Club?' You will explain to them, 'When you contribute $500, as a member of the club, you will be called upon by Governor Ogilvie from time to time for advice regarding important issues.'"

Even in 1970, $500 was nothing to these guys. The idea worked out, and I was successful recruiting these gentlemen to join the 500 Club. As a result, in two months we raised a quarter-of-a-million dollars. Actually, I was honored to be called on to do it.

At the same time, other events were transpiring. It was as if I couldn't lose—I had a "golden touch." Everything was coming together like clockwork. For example, as a member of the Senator's campaign staff, I had been recruiting volunteers as campaign workers. I was now in a bigger league. This was senatorial campaigning. Then I began to consider, *'Where are all these staff and volunteers going to work? I need to show my stuff. It's one thing to raise money, but it's another thing altogether to demonstrate that I am competent and can be trusted to get the job done.'*

Immediately, I began to visit all the different areas in the region. I looked for vacant commercial space—*any* vacant place. I didn't care where it was, as long as it was for rent. In every one of the region's key areas, I rented something, office or retail space for a campaign headquarters. I took the initiative. I asked no one's permission. To pay for all of this, I used my own personal credit card. Within a couple of days, I had acquired eight different locations all paid for with my MasterCard. Later, I was reimbursed for the charges. No one on the campaign staff had ever done this.

After that, I called the telephone company and set up phone banks for each of the headquarter locations. Prior to this senate campaign, I had no experience with any of this. But, I managed to pull it off.

I had the locations and I had the telephones, but now I needed more volunteers to man the phones. My solution was to call the other campaigns, such as for Lieutenant Governor, for Sheriff, and all the down-ticket candidates.

I was representing the top of the ticket in the upcoming election. It was 1970, and there wasn't a presidential election that year. *"You can use our phones and our campaign headquarters space for free. Send over your workers and your volunteers for*

Sheriff and Lieutenant Governor, and all the other offices. If you send them over, the rental space and the phones are all without cost to your candidate."

It worked! They supplied the manpower while I supplied telephones and the work space. Overnight, I had a campaign running. My area was the only one in the state to win against the Democrats.

Everyone was starting to believe I had the golden touch. I was also getting a reputation as Charlie's protégé. Charlie would make trips all over the country, and to foreign countries, to raise money. In some circles, he was even called a "bagman." This might not have been an exaggeration. In fact, that was an interesting aspect of his personal history—and his particular assignment in World War II.

Charlie's path from Illinois farm boy to dignitary of Standard Oil of Indiana and Republican kingmaker was a fascinating story. He was raised on an Illinois farm. After college, he graduated from law school. When WWII broke out, he joined the Army and was posted to the Judge Advocate's Corp. As a young lieutenant and attorney, he was attached to General Dwight David Eisenhower. Charlie had

> Charlie had only one function. He was responsible for the $80 million *in cash* Allied Commander General Eisenhower brought to Europe.

only one function. He was responsible for the $80 million *in cash* Allied Commander General Eisenhower brought to Europe.

Charlie believed many people underestimated General Eisenhower. Some said he was a real *Boy Scout,* a comment which was meant to be derogatory. Actually, he was a very shrewd man. For example, Eisenhower's philosophy was, *'Why fight a battle if you can buy it?'* And he did buy some battles.

11—Paul, What Do You Want?

Charlie told me of one instance, during the Italy campaign, when the Italian fleet never made it out of the harbor. They just never sailed. The right admiral was approached through a neutral third party. A sum of money was paid in advance, and an additional amount when *"results"* were achieved. This took a lot of cash—buying battles. Charlie was completely in charge of the money. He was told, *"If anyone gets near that money, you shoot him."* It was all in cash dollars.

In his capacity handling the money for General Eisenhower, Charlie met some very important people. Obviously, that carried a lot of weight. It didn't hurt Charlie's future a bit when General Dwight Eisenhower became President Eisenhower for eight years. The Vice President for the years of Eisenhower's presidency was Richard Nixon. One thing leads to another, one person leads to another, and Charlie's future in Republican politics was set.

I swiftly learned Charlie was at the top of the food chain. I then discovered there were eleven political kingmakers in the country. Of the eleven, some were previously his protégés. He had been involved in Republican politics going back to Senator Robert Taft, a conservative Senator from Ohio during the period 1939-53. Charlie earned his early political bones with Senator Taft by alerting the Senator he was about to be snookered by legislative language included in a pending bill.

Charlie explained, and then proved, the consequences to Senator Taft. From that time, Charlie was completely trusted by Senator Taft, who was the major conservative figure in the Republican Party during the late 1940s and early 1950s. Senator Taft was even a serious Presidential candidate.

Charlie was a kingmaker, but he was my close, personal friend. As a result, people started calling me when they couldn't reach Charlie. When I first started to receive calls regarding Charlie's business, it seemed peculiar to me. I learned that I was known to be Charlie's protégé and that he was my mentor. Folks thought it was logical to reach out to me when they couldn't locate Charlie.

One day I received an urgent call meant for Charlie. *"The White House is calling. We need somebody to head up HUD (Housing and Urban Development) in the Midwest. Can you give us a recommendation?"* Immediately, I contacted Charlie and passed along the message.

"All right, Paul. I'm going to be home in a few days. Make a list of possible candidates, and we'll go over your names when I see you Saturday."

When Saturday rolled around, I brought my list, and Charlie and I discussed the various candidates. After a while, he admitted he didn't like any of the names. Then he paused for a moment and looked at me. *"Paul, why don't you do it? You know, there's absolutely no reason why you couldn't do it. We'll just call back and give them your name."*

I tried to catch my breath at his suggestion. *"I don't know Charlie. It sounds . . . I don't know about this. I mean, do I know enough?"*

"A lot of people do these jobs. They don't know any more than you do."

I wasn't convinced. *"I don't know. It seems a little over my head."*

"Well, how about being a deputy?"

I made it clear—I was not up for this. Charlie was beginning to wonder about my hesitancy. *'What the heck is going on here?'* He clearly didn't understand my reluctance. Eventually, we decided on someone else. Later, I was sitting in the office with Charlie and the White House called back. *"Do you have our man yet? Who's going to be the guy?"*

11—Paul, What Do You Want?

Charlie put them off. *"We're still discussing it. Can you have someone come out here? By the time your man arrives, we'll have the name for you."* They promptly dispatched the Vice President's Air Force plane. The same afternoon, the White House assistant, Ed Herman, was in Charlie's office. This was really heady stuff— very heady stuff.

Now that I had declined an offer for both the number one and number two HUD positions, Charlie let me off the hook. *"Paul, your decision may be the smart thing. It will be the state legislature all over again. There will be a lot of contracts worth a lot of money. HUD has $4 billion worth of FHA money flowing through the system. People are going to want you to cooperate in some way. They will want to feel like they have some connection with you. Maybe it is smart you don't do that."* He had gracefully given me a reason for turning it down, which I latched onto. The truth was, I was *afraid* of accepting either position.

> **By the time your man arrives, we'll have the name for you." They promptly dispatched the Vice President's Air Force plane.**

The following week we were sitting in Charlie's car. *"Paul, I've got to ask you a question. What do you want? You've been working for me for almost two years. Where is this going? What do you want?"*

"What do you mean, Charlie? I don't want anything."

He wasn't buying my answer. *"No, tell me what you want. You didn't want either of the jobs at HUD? What do you want?"*

"Charlie I don't want anything. I am having such a great time. For someone like me to be doing all these things—I feel it is an honor and a privilege just to do what I do. I don't want anything more. I have everything I want."

11—Paul, What Do You Want?

"That's no good Paul. You have to understand something. I have a thing where I choose the people who are going to be my protégés. Over the years, there have been almost 100 people who have been my protégés. I see who is going to be successful. Then, I create a little bridge for them to walk across to help them on their way to success.

"Forever after that, I will have access and credibility because I helped them. I never ask anything in return. But, they listen to me because I helped them on their way. That's why I've mentored all these senators, congressmen, and heads of national trade associations.

"You might see by now this is a good system. It works. You have to accept something because, if I don't reward you, it will be noticed and people will not be waiting in line to be my protégé. That's why everybody wants to be my protégé, because everybody gets a good reward. So, you have to accept something.

"Paul, I see you as a leader. You are a natural born leader. I size people up and identify those people who are going to be successful. I want to be along for their success and to play a role in that accomplishment. I believe in destiny, and I believe it is your destiny to be successful. Paul, I don't know if you're going to be a candidate, or behind the scenes, but you have a real future in politics. However, you have to go on to the next stage. Tell me, Paul. What is your fantasy? What do you fantasize that you would really like to do?"

12—Washington, DC

It was the middle of October 1970 when Charlie asked me, *"What do you want?"*

I was caught off guard by the question. I had never considered it before. So, I just rolled something off the top of my head. *"You know, Charlie, a fantasy for me would be . . . I wouldn't mind going to Washington, DC."*

What I meant was, *'I wouldn't mind being a congressman.'* But that's not what came out. I had previously never considered the question, and my answer was unnecessarily vague.

"Washington, DC? Oh, we can do that. Can you be on a plane Tuesday?"

"Sure! Certainly!"

Charlie asked me the question on Saturday, and by Tuesday we were on a plane to Washington, DC.

> What I meant was, *'I wouldn't mind being a congressman.'*

He didn't understand that I wanted to be a congressman. He thought I wanted to move to Washington, DC for employment. For him, this was a matter easily resolved.

Once we arrived, we began making the rounds, visiting Charlie's friends and associates; the head of the U.S. Chamber of Commerce; the head of the National Association of Manufacturers, and many others. As Charlie introduced me to these men, he was keeping his eyes and ears open for a career opportunity for me.

Charlie was my guy. He was taking me around Washington because Charlie Barr helped many of these people to attain their positions in government and public service. Some of these men already were established with solid careers when they first met him, but Charlie helped them move up the ladder. They *owed* him, and when Charlie called, their doors were always open.

Then we headed over to the Commerce Department to meet another *"friend"* by the name of Dr. Robert Miller. We were chatting when Charlie began to tell the guy some of the things I had accomplished in Chicago, as well as our purpose in Washington, DC. This fellow was freshly installed in the Commerce Department.

"Charlie, right now I am forming my policy group. Paul, you strike me as a policy kind of person. I have ten areas to develop for the Office of Domestic Business Policy. You seem to be a man who likes conceptual things. It looks like a fit to me." On the spot, he offered me a position with the Commerce Department, and I accepted without hesitation.

As we were leaving, Charlie's contact told me, *"Paul, we'll be in touch."*

Charlie had done *his* job. He had secured a position for me in Washington, DC. We were ready to head back to Chicago.

As soon as we arrived back in Chicago, I rushed home to tell Susan. *"We're moving. I have a job in Washington, DC at the Commerce Department. We're putting the house up for sale."* As always, Susan didn't want to hold me back. We're going. That was it. She trusted me.

When I told my father, he was skeptical. It was as if, *'We'll believe it when we see it.'* But no one at work really believed that I would just pull up stakes and move.

I assured them it was true. *"I have the job. We have an agreement."* I didn't have anything in writing, but Charlie's transactions were reliable. To someone from the outside who didn't know the way things worked and hadn't been involved, it didn't sound very concrete.

Then things hit a snag. The house was up for sale, but there were *no* buyers. *'What are we going to do?'* September came and went and then October, but there were no offers. Nobody was offering to buy the house. At the same time, I hadn't heard from anyone at the Commerce Department.

I finally gave up, took the sign down and withdrew the house from the market. My reasoning was, *'I tried. Fine. I'll just keep working Rich Township for the Republican Party, and I'll keep working with Charlie. Washington, DC just didn't work out. It just wasn't meant to be.'*

The Thanksgiving holiday came and I was sick with the flu. When Sunday of Thanksgiving weekend arrived, I was upstairs in bed feeling like death warmed over. I looked as bad as I felt. I had not even shaved. From my bed, I heard the doorbell downstairs. Susan answered the door, and I could overhear bits of the conversation. *"We're looking for a home to buy. We know yours used to be for sale."*

I heard this discussion downstairs and it got me thinking. *'How unusual—the house is no longer for sale, there is no sign, and we no longer have a realtor. Now these people come to the front door to inquire whether or not my house is for sale. Bingo! Something is going on here!'*

At the same moment, I remembered the Jesus psychic's prediction. *'I'll be in my new house by Christmas.'* By now, I was already comfortable with the idea that I was getting help from somewhere. *'Everything up to now has worked out, right?'*

All these thoughts were running through my mind when I heard Susan. *"No, I'm sorry, but it's no longer for sale."* I jumped out of bed in my pajamas, ran downstairs, and interrupted. *"We should*

I remembered the Jesus psychic's prediction. *'I'll be in my new house by Christmas.'*

talk. If the price is right, then yes, this house is for sale. Can I ask why you are coming to our house? I mean, it's a tract home, and there are a lot of houses with our same floor plan that are available."

"We are aware, but yours is right across from the school. We don't want our children to have to walk too far to cross the streets on their way to class. Plus, your particular model is the floor plan we prefer. Also, we really like what you did with the exterior and in your front yard."

What they said made sense, so I got right to the bottom line. *"What about the price? It has to be $45,000. Okay?"* The house we bought for $33,000 was now valued at $45,000.

They were in agreement with the price, but they had a request. *"We have a problem. We can pay you your price if you can solve our problem. We have sold our home, and we absolutely must be out of that house by December 22. If we can move into your house on the 22nd of December, we'll pay you your price."*

This was happening very fast. I needed to step back and catch my breath. *"I'll let you know by tomorrow. I promise I will call you, one way or the other, whatever we decide."*

First thing the next morning, Monday, I was on the phone with the Commerce Department in Washington, DC. I was put through to the assistant for Robert Miller, Charlie's contact who had hired me. *"Do I still have a job? Are you still offering me the job? I haven't received any paperwork about it."*

"Oh Yes, Mr. Liberman. We've put through your paperwork. We simply haven't yet received a response, but that's not unusual. You know how bureaucracies are. I realize we should have been pursuing it. However, we are expecting you to arrive here."

"That's great because I have a buyer for my house. Today, I'm going to accept their offer."

The guy started to stutter a bit. *"You know, Mr. Liberman, you really should wait for the government paperwork. Otherwise, you could sell your home and arrive here in Washington, DC, and . . ."*

He was trying to slow me down. At the same time, I'm thinking, *'This is destiny! It's predicted!'* So I told the guy, *"No! I'm not waiting any longer. I'm doing this on my own hook. I'm coming. You can expect me."*

That same day, we accepted the couple's offer on our home. Immediately after the offer was accepted, I began calling Washington, DC realtors who were listed in the yellow pages. I called a number of people until I settled on one that seemed like the best choice, and I explained our situation to him.

"I will be there Friday with my wife, and we need to find a house right away. By Sunday night we are leaving, and you will have our name on the dotted line. Line up everything that has the following specifications . . ."

Susan's mother offered to babysit with the kids, and that same week Susan and I were on an airplane to Washington, DC. By the time we arrived that Friday, the realtor had lined up 27 homes that met our specifications.

We drove to the first one on the list, looked at the front, and didn't even get out of the car. *"No, that's not it."*

We quickly made our way down the list and around town. *"No, that's not it."*

"No, that's not the one."

"Not that one either."

We were getting close to the last house on his list—maybe the 26th home out of 27. I already had a sort of mental visualization of the house we were looking for and this was it! It was exactly what we had pictured our home would look like. It was on a hill. It had pillars in the front. It was perfect!

During this entire tour, Susan was sort of turning her nose up at everything. As soon as we arrived at this particular house, she got out of the car, walked through the front door, into the interior, and stared. *"Paul, this is a beautiful home."* And I thought, *'That's it. The way she said, "This is a beautiful home." She has never said that about any other house before this one.'*

The asking price was $69,000. I quickly calculated that with the $15,000 we were getting from the sale of our house in Chicago, there would be enough for a down payment. The rest would

'The way she said, "This is a beautiful home." She has never said that about any other house before this one.'

have to be covered by a mortgage. We could just get into this house. I told the realtor, *"When would the closing take place? We need to do this right away if we're going to."*

The realtor inquired with a phone call and brought back the verdict. *"Mr. Liberman, closing either has to be on the 24th of December, or it cannot be until January 10th. The builder is going to be in Florida for the holidays."*

"Then it has to be the 24th. Otherwise, what am I going to do with my family? Where are they going to stay?" With that settled, we signed the contract, and we had a deal.

Before the closing date, on the 22nd, I drove our little car all the way from Chicago to Washington, DC. Susan stayed with the kids at her mother's. In a new city, with some effort, on the morning of the 24th of December, I found the lawyer's office where the closing was scheduled to occur. We finished signing the last of the paperwork, and all of the settlement documents were executed. Once we were completely done, I asked the question I'd been pondering since Susan and I signed the purchase contract. *"Am I correct that, if I make these payments, nobody can take this house away from me, no matter what? Is that true?"*

"Mr. Liberman, the house is yours, no matter what. It is all signed, sealed and delivered. Nothing can undo this."

That is when I popped the question I'd been wondering about ever since we signed the contract with the realtor. *"That's very good. Let me ask you another question. When it came time to obtain the mortgage, how did I get the loan?"* I was wondering whether the bank attempted to call the Commerce Department and, if so, what was said.

"Mr. Liberman, you remember you were in such a hurry to close that we had to walk this transaction through in order to accomplish everything in time. The officer at the lender's office, Jefferson National Bank, told us, 'There is certainly no need to check out the man's employment. It's obvious he's getting the job at the Commerce Department, or he wouldn't be moving here.'"

It was Christmas Eve when I unlocked the door to our new home. The floors were bare, except for some newspapers scattered around. There was no furniture. I began to ponder the events of the previous

> *"It's obvious he's getting the job at the Commerce Department, or he wouldn't be moving here."*

twelve months. *'My goodness—how could you predict something like this? It must be that events are programmed in advance—in detail. I really need to understand more about this destiny thing and how it works.'*

13—Chance Meeting–Congress to the Rescue

A few days passed between Christmas and New Year's Day. I found myself sitting in an empty house with nothing to do but wrestle with the entire concept of destiny. I concluded that I wanted to learn everything I could about prophecy and destiny. *'How could someone such as the psychic lady predict all this? There's no sense or probability to explain it. There has to be something more going on. What about the entire political thing that led up to our coming to Washington, DC? What about the sale of the house in Chicago after it was off the market? And, the way we found the perfect house in Washington, DC, with the mortgage coming through in less than two weeks, without an employment verification. How would anyone explain all this? I just have to know—how does it work?'*

Finally, Susan, the children, and the furniture arrived. There was plenty to keep me busy—fixing up the house, hanging pictures, and putting our personal items away. It had not escaped my notice that I hadn't yet received any paperwork from the Commerce Department. After a couple of weeks passed, I began to wonder, *'What am I going to do? There's really nothing more for me to do around this house. I know, this is Washington, DC. I will go sightseeing.'*

It was February 1, 1971. I headed up to the Capitol and wandered around, just looking at all the government buildings, wondering what to do next. As I

> **I ran right into Congressmen Ed Derwinski from Chicago's 4th District. I had worked for him on one of Charlie's projects.**

strolled down the steps of the Capitol, I ran right into Congressmen Ed Derwinski from Chicago's 4th District. I had worked for him on one of Charlie's projects. *"Hey Paul! It's great to see you! What are you doing here in Washington, DC?"*

13—Chance Meeting–Congress to the Rescue

I was pleased to have someone to talk to. I told him the entire story about coming to Washington with Charlie and about being hired at the Commerce Department. *"So, have you started to work yet?"*

"Not exactly—I'm still waiting for the official paperwork."

He stared at me for a moment. *"What are you waiting for?"*

"You know. I'm waiting for a telephone call, or an official letter to come, or something to tell me to start work."

He had a troubled look in his face. *"You moved here from Chicago with your family, and you still don't have anything in writing?"*

I assured him this was indeed the case. At that moment, his face stiffened, and resolve took over. *"Paul, I want you to go home right now. I will call you tonight about 6:30. We're going to see to this matter, okay?"*

That evening, Congressmen Derwinski called me at my house. *"Paul, I have the Commerce Department on the other line. We've been talking for some while about you. They have found your paperwork. I told them, 'Mr. Paul Liberman is a personal friend of mine. He has moved here from Chicago because he received an employment offer. Why haven't you people performed on your commitment? Now you have the paperwork. I'll just hang on the line until you work through those documents.'"*

By the time the Congressman called me, he had already been on the phone for over ninety minutes. He made it clear to the bureaucrat at Commerce that the congressman wasn't getting off the phone until the Commerce Department did what was right and resolved the injustice done to Mr. Paul Liberman! I could hear him speaking on the other line. Then, he turned his attention to me. *"Okay, Paul, tomorrow you show up for work."*

I hung up from that call and right away began to marvel. *'What are the chances I'm going to walk right into this particular congressman that I happen to know? I'm walking down the steps of the Capitol building, being a tourist, and just at the moment, he's walking in. What the heck is going on here? This is surreal!'*

The next day, February 2, I showed up at the Commerce Department for my first day as a government employee. I was in the waiting room for a while, when a lady came in with a clipboard and some paperwork. *"Sign here, and right here, then initial right here. Okay, Mr. Liberman. You will be a day-to-day consultant until the paperwork makes its way through the process."*

What a relief. I was now a per-diem consultant at a rate of $100 per day. It occurred to me, however, that this all seemed to be a strange arrangement for a man who was supposed to have a job.

Meanwhile, I was directed to the corner of a large open office area. After a while, Robert Miller, the guy who hired me on my first visit with Charlie Barr, came over and greeted me. His department was the *Office of Domestic Business Policy* for the Nixon administration.

"Listen, Paul, Maurice Stans, the Secretary of Commerce, has been asked to put on a White House conference with a theme of 'The Industrial World ahead, 1990,' which is unquestionably long-range thinking. The task of organizing this has fallen to the Commerce Department, and I have been put in charge of this conference. Paul, you've come in off the campaign trail. You're

> **"Paul, Maurice Stans, the Secretary of Commerce, has been asked to put on a White House conference with a theme of 'The Industrial World ahead, 1990'"**

a political guy. You're used to doing this kind of project. Why don't you get to work and produce an outline of how this is all supposed to work. That will be your assignment until your paperwork comes through."

I had never been to a White House conference. Nobody that I *knew* had been to a White House conference. Now, I was given a room to myself at the Commerce Department where I was supposed to dream up the steps for organizing one. After a time, I produced an outline: *'How to put on a White House conference.'* Apparently, it would later turn out, I came up with some pretty good ideas, but I was simply making them up out of my head. I had nothing to go by.

14—The Bus Ride

Before we moved from Chicago to Washington, DC, we struggled so much to get into our first home that Susan said, *"Listen Paul, if you're going to move me across the country, then we have to have a house equal to the one we're giving up in Homewood, Illinois—not an apartment anymore."*

What she said made sense. *'She's making quite a number of sacrifices. This should be a move up.'*

The house we eventually bought was in a prosperous neighborhood of Northern Virginia. However, it was an hour's drive along a very congested highway to get into the city of Washington, DC. People did not have much of an appetite for doing that every day, and I was no exception.

The first night that I spent in the house, before Susan and the kids arrived and before there was furniture, a welcoming neighbor introduced herself and offered assistance answering any questions about the community. This was certainly helpful to me. That first evening, as she was about to leave, she said offhandedly, "By the way Paul —there is a bus that comes into our area." And so, I looked for it.

Once again, Susan and I had stretched the limits of our budget to buy a house. I did the math. Parking was very expensive inside the federal triangle, plus the cost of gas added to the long drive through traffic—the bus was the better deal.

This was not a city bus, but a charter bus ridden by 30 or 40 executives. Everyone on the bus was an executive, professional, or government worker. We would all stand at different corners in the neighborhood, and we would get picked up by this bus. In the evening, the bus would pick up the same people at various corners inside the Beltway and return us to our own neighborhoods. It was a very nice arrangement—nothing shabby.

Of course, when you're doing this every day, you're seeing the same familiar faces. One guy especially caught my attention. I could see that he was a regular, everyday reading a Bible, which was unusual. He was reading the Bible, plus he was lit up at the end of an hour's ride.

This really peaked my interest. I couldn't figure it out. *'What the heck does he think is so funny?'* The other guys were giving him a terrible razzing *"Here comes Holy Joe!"* One morning on the way into the city, when I got on there was an empty seat next to him. So, I made a point to sit next to him. For one thing, he was being scoffed at, and I didn't care for that.

Also, I was curious. The radical change in my life over the past months—the quick elevator up as a result of politics—was too much for me to think it was only chance. I was eager to find out more. *'How does this destiny thing work? Maybe he's got something to explain to me.'*

So, I sat down next to him and introduced myself. His name was Cleyburn McCauley, but he went by Ray. He was an attorney and a retired Army Lieutenant Colonel, working for a private law firm in Washington, DC. *"Listen, Ray, I see these guys are making fun of you, and you don't seem to mind. I just wanted you to know, there are probably other people, like me, who wouldn't scoff at you. I wanted to let you know that. I've personally had some really extraordinary things happen that tell me there's something more going on, beyond what I can see. I don't yet understand how it works, but there is a matter of destiny, I am certain."*

I went on to relate a few of the odd experiences that led to my leaving Chicago and taking a new job in Washington, DC. I did not hold back, but told him I was certain destiny was a fact, and I truly desired to understand how it all worked. I admitted I was curious about his Bible reading and wondered whether there were answers in it that I was looking for.

"Oh yes, Paul, there definitely are. It's in this book–the Bible–all over the place. There is an entire supernatural universe all around us. You can learn a lot about the spiritual world through the Bible. And Paul, there's power in it to get things done."

Now he really had my curiosity engaged. *"Okay Ray, so explain to me something about this."*

"Paul, you said your name is 'Liberman?' So you're Jewish. All of these men in the Bible were Jewish, the descendants of Abraham, Isaac, and Jacob, just like you. But Paul, it's not just individuals who have a destiny. Nations and even cities have destinies as well."

I was definitely intrigued. I had read very little of the Holy Scriptures since I finished with Hebrew School. *"Well, that all makes sense."*

"Since you're Jewish, you will probably be interested in all the predictions that have come true in our lifetime pertaining to Israel." At that point, he opened his Bible and began to actually show me predictions.

Isaiah 66:8 (KJV)

Who hath heard such a thing? Who hath seen such things?
Shall the earth be made to bring forth in one day? *Or* shall
a nation be born at once? For as soon as Zion travailed,
she brought forth her children.

"Paul, for almost two thousand years there was no Jewish nation. On November 29, 1947, the United Nations voted to partition Palestine, clearing the way for the birth of the modern Jewish state of Israel. Then, on May 14, 1948, the same day the British evacuated Palestine, the modern Jewish state of Israel was born—in a single day—just as Isaiah predicted thousands of years before!"

"Here's another one in Isaiah."

Isaiah 35:1 (KJV)

> The wilderness and the solitary place shall be glad for
> them; and the desert shall rejoice, and blossom as the
> rose.

*"For centuries, the land of Palestine was controlled by, and
was a part of, the Ottoman Empire. During that time, up until the
20th century, it was truly a land of the desert and the swamp. Once
the Jewish people started to return to Palestine, just as predicted
in other biblical prophecies, the desert literally began to blossom
as a rose. Today, the fruit and vegetables grown in this former
'desert' supply much of Europe."*

Although Ray was pointing out the Scriptures to me, he made
me take the Bible and read the words for myself, so I could see this
was, indeed, what the Bible said. I was aware many Jews would
have been bothered by this Christian—Gentile—Bible. But, Ray
was a Gentile, so, why *wouldn't* he be showing me out of a
Christian Bible? It didn't bother me. I was just after the truth—
wherever it could be found.

*"Now, Paul, here is a really interesting prophecy in
Zephaniah."*

Zephaniah 3:9 (KJV)

> For then will I turn to the people a pure language, that
> they may all call upon the name of the LORD, to serve
> him with one consent.

*"Paul, do you know what makes a pure language? Living
languages are continually changing. For example, there is no such
thing as pure English. Every day, new idioms, expressions and
colloquialisms are created—even new words. Only a dead
language is pure. And, only once in all of history has a dead—
pure—language been restored as a living language! That is
Hebrew, which became the national language of the modern state
of Israel. After 2,000 years of Hebrew being a language of prayer*

and of study, the dead, pure language was restored to a living, national language!"

"Look at another prophecy in Isaiah."

Isaiah 11:12 (KJV)

And he shall set up an ensign for the nations, and shall assemble the outcasts of Israel, and gather together the dispersed of Judah from the four corners of the earth.

"Paul, the Jews that live in Israel today—where did they come from? I mean, there are many that were born in Israel, but today, in 1971, the majority were born where?"

"Well, the Jews have come to Israel from all over the world. After World War II, the refugees from every corner of Europe began to make their way there. Plus, after 1948, they came from every Arab country in Africa and the Middle East. I suppose there's not a place in the world from which the Jews have not come to Israel, except maybe Iceland."

"Exactly, Paul! For thousands of years there has not been a Jewish nation, yet the Jews have maintained their identity, even in exile! There is no other example of anything like that in world history! Once a people are conquered, scattered, and subjugated they are absorbed! Yet, the Bible says that God would restore the outcasts of Judah—the Jews—from the four corners of the earth! At the time of that prediction, the Jews were concentrated ONLY in the land of Israel! Yet, Isaiah not only predicts the scattering to the four corners of the globe, but ALSO predicts their return to the land of Israel! And that has happened in our lifetime!"

He was showing me these things in his Bible that were written thousands of years ago, but I was reading about things that have happened within my lifetime. I was fascinated with these ancient prophecies relating to Israel.

"The Bible goes further than saying the Jewish people will return to Israel. Look at this verse in Amos."

Amos 9:14-15 (KJV)

> [14] And I will bring again the captivity of my people of Israel, and they shall build the waste cities, and inhabit *them*; and they shall plant vineyards, and drink the wine thereof; they shall also make gardens, and eat the fruit of them.
>
> [15] And I will plant them upon their land, and they shall no more be pulled up out of their land which I have given them, saith the LORD thy God.

"Now that the Jews are back in Israel, the Bible says they will never again be pulled up or removed from their land. That is a promise."

All of this took some time. Ray had quite a repertoire of verses, and we read them together; he just didn't tell me about them. He had his Bible open, and he wanted me to read them for myself rather than taking his word for it, which I was happy to do.

At some point, I stopped him. *"Every religion says they have the answers. What makes the Bible so special?"*

"Paul, the answer to that question is one word—prophecy. You need to understand the importance of prophecy. Prophecy is what really distinguishes the Bible from all other religions. According to the Bible, prophecy is the great authenticator. The Bible is filled with hundreds, if not thousands, of specific predictions, many of which have already been accurately fulfilled.

"As the prophet Isaiah points out, only an all-knowing and all-powerful, Eternal God, could accurately predict events decades, and even centuries, in advance. None of the other world's religions have this kind of predictive prophecy. It's not a manmade contrivance. Fulfilled prophecy proves the Bible is supernatural."

As Ray was making this point about prophecy, we were pulling into the Federal Triangle. The time had really flown by. Once he started on the idea of prophecy, I thought, *'Oh, this is it! This is gonna give me a clue.'*

15—In the Soup

I started to work at the Commerce Department on February 2, 1971. Within the first 30 days, Robert Miller, the guy who hired me, was fired. It soon became obvious the reason my paperwork hadn't gone through was they *knew* they were going to fire him. I started to put these facts together in my head: no paperwork; a per-diem consultant, not a regular job; the guy who hired me had been fired ... I was left with a sinking feeling in my stomach. That same day when I got home, I called Charlie Barr to tell him what had happened.

Charlie didn't mince words. *"Paul, you are in the soup. I know this is going to start playing with your head, so I want you to call me every single day, including Saturdays and Sundays, until this is resolved. I want to know how you're doing."*

Mostly, Charlie was being a good friend. He just wanted to keep my spirits up, but it was *more* than that. I could not fail! If one of Charlie's guys failed, it would mark him in a very public and negative way. He had already explained that. Charlie was a big shot. He talked to presidents, and now he was looking out for *me*.

In the meantime, I was a day-to-day consultant. I *was* getting paid, so I tried not to worry too much. Things seemed to be working out. I was soon given another assignment with another supervisor. My new job had to do with legislation.

I had an assignment designator. I was doing the work of a *legislative analyst,* writing the Commerce Department's opinion on various pieces of proposed business legislation. Every day, I went up to Capitol Hill and sat in on the hearings. But, I was still not a regular employee. I was a per-diem consultant.

15—In the Soup

I was on a staff with others. Our task was to comment on proposed legislation on behalf of the Nixon administration. At the Commerce Department, we would receive requests to comment on prospective legislation from various committees of the Congress. In some cases, the committees would write to the Commerce Department or, in other cases, they contacted the White House. Whether they wrote to the White

> I was doing the work of a *legislative analyst,* writing the Commerce Department's opinion on various pieces of proposed business legislation. Every day, I went up to Capitol Hill and sat in on the hearings.

House or the Commerce Department, it would funnel into us, and our staff would take the first pass at writing a response letter reflecting the Nixon Administration's position.

To accomplish this, we would call upon the various lobbying groups to catch both sides of the issue. Afterward, we would draft correspondence outlining a position. This draft would float up through channels for approval and changes, all before a congressional committee would seriously consider the proposal.

16—Do You Have an Altar in Your Backyard?

I had been thinking a lot about my first conversation on the bus with Ray McCauley. I'd already decided, *'I've got to sit next to him again. He knows more. I have to find out how this destiny thing works.'*

A few days passed, and I kept my eye out for him. One rainy afternoon, after work, I met the bus to catch my ride home and there was Ray McCauley. So, again, I sat down next to this interesting guy. This time, he was waiting for me with a whole new agenda besides prophecies from the Bible about Israel.

We exchanged greetings, and then Ray opened the second conversation. *"Paul, there's a lot more to the Bible than prophecies. There's other stuff in here that's of interest besides Israel. I can keep going on about Israel, but you get the idea. Do you know what the Bible is really about? Under it all, it really has to do with moral issues. On a moral plane, have you led a sinless life, Paul?"*

What did he expect me to say? *"Well, you know, uh . . ."*

"What are you gonna do about getting into Heaven, Paul?"

"I guess, like everyone else, I'm gonna be a good guy and hope for the best."

"Unfortunately, that's not good enough. Do you remember, Paul, for your ancestors there was a whole Temple process that was necessary for relating to God. And before the Temple,

> *"What are you gonna do about getting into Heaven, Paul?"*
> *"I guess, like everyone else, I'm gonna be a good guy and hope for the best."*

there was the Tabernacle. Let me show you a verse from the Torah in Leviticus that is a key Scripture for understanding all of this."

16—Do You Have an Altar in Your Backyard?

Leviticus 17:11 (KJV)

> For the life of the flesh is in the blood: and I have given it to you upon the altar to make an atonement for your souls: for it is the blood that maketh an atonement for the soul.

"To be at one with God, He says it will take the blood of atonement. Here is the point. Paul, have you led a perfect life?"

I was suddenly very uncomfortable with the direction this conversation was heading. *"Well, you know . . ."*

"Paul, what are you doing about the fact that this Temple no longer exists where you were commanded to make these sacrifices?"

As soon as he started talking about sacrifices, I was getting fidgety, but I was going along with it. *"Uh . . . You know."*

"Of course, maybe you have an altar in your backyard. Are you doing this—offering a sacrifice?" he said tongue in cheek. *"Paul, do you have an altar in your backyard?"*

"No, of course not."

Then what are you doing about this necessity for sacrifices?"

There was a really uncomfortable pause because I didn't know what he expected me to say. *'Where is this conversation going, and what does this have to do with destiny?'*

"Fortunately Paul, this book – the Bible – is written supernaturally, and it has the answer to the sacrifice issue. There is an answer to this dilemma. It's an old problem, but it still exists even today. The answer is contained in the ancient Jewish concept of a Messiah. "

Suddenly, I knew where he was going. I felt myself begin to tense up inside. I am pretty sure he's going to talk to me about the New Testament. I have zero curiosity to hear it. And I'm no longer interested in seeing or talking to this man, ever again.

16—Do You Have an Altar in Your Backyard?

"Do you have a blood sacrifice, Paul, because Leviticus clearly says you require one? Fortunately, there was one made on your behalf. Take a look at what the prophet Isaiah has to say about this subject in chapter 53."

At this point, he began to read from his Bible again, and all I could think about was planning for my escape.

I am pretty sure he's going to talk to me about the New Testament. I have zero curiosity to hear it.

"But he was wounded for our transgressions, he was bruised for our iniquities: the chastisement of our peace was upon him."

Only the smallest bit of what he was reading or saying was coming through, but I'd had about enough.

"All we like sheep have gone astray; we have turned every one, to his own way; and the Lord hath laid on him the iniquity of us all . . . for he was cut off out of the land of the living: for the transgression of my people was he stricken."

'Here I was just trying to be nice to the guy, and he's taking liberties, trying to rearrange my head with his propaganda.'

"Yet it pleased the Lord to bruise him . . . when thou shalt make his soul an offering for sin . . . by his knowledge shall my righteous servant justify many; for he shall bear their iniquities . . . and he bare the sin of many, and made intercession for the transgressors."

My discomfort was becoming increasingly obvious. However, I think he was prepared for me to be offended, because he pulled out another book and passed it to me—*Messiah in Both Testaments*, by Fred John Meldau. It claimed to contain over 300 Old Testament Messianic prophecies and their fulfillments.

16—Do You Have an Altar in Your Backyard?

As Ray handed it to me, I was already getting out of my seat. I had made the decision to get off the bus without any further delay. I'd had enough! But I took his booklet.

"Paul, if you want to know more about this, it's all in here—all the prophecies about the coming Messiah are here. You'll have to decide if this Jesus was the Messiah or if you're still waiting for another one.

'Here I was just trying to be nice to the guy, and he's taking liberties, trying to rearrange my head with his propaganda.'

Whomever it's gonna be, whether it's Jesus or someone else, he is going to have to fit this prescription as prophesied in the Jewish Bible–the Old Testament."

I was standing up to get off, but he was still talking to me. All I could think about was getting off that bus! That was it! *'Enough already!'* I pulled the cord hard to stop the bus. It wasn't a regular stop, and it certainly wasn't mine. The driver had to make an unscheduled stop. I hastily ran down the steps and exited as fast as I could.

Once I was off the bus, I was immediately soaked in the rain, and I was still several blocks from my house! Even in good weather, it would have been a long walk—but this was ridiculous! Our neighborhood was not exactly the plains of Middle America. It seemed uphill all the way.

As I ran to my house, I was furious! I was angry that he'd taken liberties. I was just trying to be nice to the guy, and he had taken advantage, trying to rearrange my head with his Gentile propaganda! As I was jogging on the sidewalk in the drenching rain, I remember thinking, *'Oh, I hope he's wrong!'*

17—The Book and the Bible

Ray McCauley had posed a totally ridiculous question to me on the ride home. *"Paul, do you have an altar in your back yard?"* He was saying that since there was no longer a Jewish Temple in which to offer sacrifices, there was no offering for sins. His solution, naturally, was to suggest the Gentile alternative—Jesus! I felt so violated with his heavy-handed proposal, that I halted the bus blocks from my usual stop and escaped into the driving rain.

As I removed my wet clothes and changed for dinner, I resolved never to take the bus again. I wasn't about to permit a repeat performance. Susan recognized something was bothering me, but I wasn't ready to discuss it. I deflected her questions, mumbling something about work.

After dinner, I excused myself and pulled out the book Ray had plunged into my hand. In spite of the weather, somehow the book had managed to stay dry. I determined that it wasn't enough to *hope* he was wrong, I needed to know for sure. What harm could it do to read his 100-page booklet?

As I opened it up, I repeated to myself, what I'd said wading home in the rain. *'I hope he's wrong!'* But, almost immediately, I was hooked. I had barely started reading when I came to the words that nailed it for me.

> ***Fulfilled Prophecy Is Unique to the Bible****–The fact of fulfilled prophecy is found in the Bible alone; hence, it presents proof of Divine inspiration that is positive, conclusive, overwhelming. Here is the argument in brief: no man, unaided by Divine inspiration, foreknows the future, for it is an impenetrable wall, a true "iron curtain," to all mankind. Only an almighty and an all-knowing God can infallibly predict the future. If then one can find true prophecy (as one does in the Bible), with definite fulfillment, with sufficient time intervening between the*

prediction and the fulfillment, and with explicit details in the prediction to assure that the prophecies are not clever guesses, then the case is perfect and unanswerable.

Remember, there were 400 years between the last of the Messianic predictions of the Old Testament and their fulfillment in the Christ of the Gospels. Many prophecies are of course much older than 400 B.C. During the period of 1100 years, from the age of Moses (1500 B.C.) to that of Malachi (400 B.C.), a succession of prophets arose, Messianic prediction took form, and all of them testified of the Messiah who was to come.[1]

I did read his book. I read it cover to cover, and I was trapped. There was just no wiggle room at all. Once I was past 5, 10, 20 specific prophecies about who the Messiah was going to be . . . then, there were many more intricate prophecies. To fit this prescription, I was satisfied there was no way possible it could be anything other than supernatural. It was indisputable. That left me thinking, *'I'm the only Jewish guy on the face of the earth who has come to this conclusion. I'm really alone.'* The implications were extremely unsettling. I didn't know what to do with this information, but I knew I couldn't ignore it.

I resolved I was not taking the bus anymore. One of the reasons I signed up for the charter service was that we

'I'm the only Jewish guy on the face of the earth who has come to this conclusion. I'm really alone.'

really didn't have the money to own two cars. We had one little Toyota, and that was when Toyotas were very cheap. I believe we paid $2,500 total, and we made payments on that amount. We had no extra money. The bus helped us avoid requiring another vehicle. If I wasn't prepared to take the bus, I needed to buy another auto. The solution—I bought my mother-in-law's car for $300, an old Ford. After that, I drove to work.

Once I had my transportation worked out, I had two hours a day of commuting time to ponder the booklet and sometimes to listen to Christian radio. That's also when I decided I wanted to read—I had to read—the Bible for myself. *'Okay, I have to look more into this.'*

I was only interested in the New Testament. I believed I had a working knowledge of the Old Testament. However, the sanctions from boyhood about "this Jesus guy" were still with me. It was very clear from my days in Orthodox Hebrew School, *"If you read the New Testament, you are going to Hell when you die. In this life, all kinds of bad things happen to Jews who read it!"* That was the way I was trained in my synagogue. To overcome this prohibition, I first had to be somewhat of an agnostic or atheist. That was just to have enough courage to be willing to read the New Testament.

Once I made the decision I was going to read this Gentile Bible, I had to settle on a strategy as to where and how I would find a New Testament. I wasn't about to buy one. I wasn't going to carry a Bible around Capitol Hill. I was always visiting with people, and everyone knew I was Jewish. I really didn't want anyone seeing me, especially Susan.

That problem was easily resolved. My job duties required me to monitor congressional hearings nearly every day. Then I would give a report to my bureaucratic superiors at the Commerce Department. That offered me a lot of freedom. At lunchtime there were no hearings, so I went across the street to the Library of Congress where I was quite sure I could find a Christian Bible.

I went into the stacks, careful that nobody I knew should see me, and began reading the New Testament. I barricaded myself behind the piles of books so that no one would see me reading this provocative text; the one no self-respecting Jew should ever be reading.

For a Jewish man like me, the idea of reading the New Testament was so far out, so strange, it was positively distasteful.

It wouldn't be an exaggeration to say it was inconceivable. I was aware I was unquestionably doing it on the sneak. I was sneaking. I was sneaking into the Library of Congress and I was sneaking over to where I had found a New Testament. I had a feeling of sneaking in, so that no one should see me.

First, I read one of the Gospel accounts, trying to find out why it is that the Jewish people do not recognize Jesus as the Messiah. I was thinking, *'There are so many fulfilled prophecies. Why have the Jewish sages—all the rabbis over the years—why are they so angry with this Jesus?'*

I needed to know why. After I read one of the Gospels, I really *liked* this Jesus fellow. There was nothing about Him I *didn't* like. And, I could not see anything—any reason—why anyone should be upset with Him. He was a good guy all the way. So much antipathy for so long and the prejudice against Him and his followers—it really puzzled me. The slanders—I just couldn't see it.

And, the Gospels were told in a totally Jewish context. I was aware of the fact I was reading the New Testament, which is supposed to be a Gentile book. But, I'm reading a story whose context is totally Jewish. This was confusing. It was definitely not what I was expecting. Except for the name—*Jesus*— I felt I was reading a Jewish story. There was nothing in that first Gospel story that was foreign to me. Everything about it was telling me the history of my people.

---

[1] Fred John Meldau, *Messiah in Both Testaments* (Denver: The Christian Victory Publishing Company, 1967), p. 5

18—Parking Lot Prayer

March 5 was my Bar Mitzvah Day. This date was always special to me. In 1971, it fell on a Friday, which was about a week after my second encounter with Ray McCauley. The time since found me struggling with unresolved inner turmoil.

First, my job situation was still very much up in the air. I was hanging on as a per diem consultant, but the uncertainty was doing a number on my head.

As if that wasn't enough, the second encounter with Ray McCauley and his book had left me with a considerable quandary. In order to settle this dilemma, I made what seemed to be a perfectly rational decision to search for a copy of the New Testament and see for myself. I found one at the Library of Congress. Instead of resolving anything, this quest for facts led me further into what appeared to be a proverbial box canyon—one way in and no way out.

I had never considered myself a person who questioned his own identity. I knew who I was—a Jew—part of a people with an enduring history going back centuries to biblical times. When I started asking questions about "destiny" and "prophecy," I wasn't really sure what I expected, but I was *certain* I hadn't expected to come face-to-face with the Gentile's Jesus!

If I believed what Ray's book said—if I accepted what this New Testament was saying—the questions I was asking and the answers I claimed I was seeking were leading me to a Messiah I hadn't even known I required. This was becoming personal.

I took my lunch into the Library of Congress and read some more of the New Testament. When I finally closed the book, I went to an outdoor parking lot and began to pace. For me, this was now my own private island in the midst of pandemonium. There, I began to walk and to speak out loud to God. (I wanted to be sure that He heard me.)

"God, I'm very confused about all this. Is this Gentile propaganda, or is it the truth? I'm very confused about it, and I don't know what's going to clarify it for me, 'cause I can't really discuss it with anybody. If you are God, You ought to be able to straighten out my confusion.

Also, I really would appreciate some help at the Commerce Department, because I'm in a very insecure position. You gotta see my situation here. I'm sure You've

> *"God, I'm very confused about all this. Is this Gentile propaganda, or is it the truth?"*

noticed I'm having a great deal of problems because the guy who hired me got fired. I can't get the paperwork through, and I'm a day-to-day, per diem consultant. I have to go in every night to find out whether I can come to work the next morning. I'm sure You know that's an uneasy existence. You gotta help me out here.

And, as regards all this Jesus business—if this Jesus is the Messiah—if he is the Messiah and the answer to all these prophecies, I need a Messiah for my situation, and I need him right away. I want him to be my Messiah. Okay? Cause, the way it looks to me, nobody can help me except a Messiah. Take over—however it works, take over."

I didn't know the lingo, but almost immediately I felt a kind of release. Then, I began to reason with myself, *'If He can't hear that, He can't hear anything and there's no point ever praying at all for anything. So, if my prayer is not answered, then I'm free to live a hedonistic life, completely. That's it, either way I win. If God can't answer that very sincere prayer, then I was right in the first place; there is no God. Or certainly the universe is a windup toy. On the other hand, if He does answer my prayer, then okay. Now I've got some kind of a foundation going here. This is a win-win situation.'*

I decided to sit back and relax. For me, it was settled.

19—Nice Jewish Boy to Agnostic

There are two things we American Jews have in abundance—doctors and analysts. We love our doctors: whether it is raising them or visiting them. And, we have our analysts. One of the perks of the leisurely life in America for the successful Jewish adult is the right to enjoy a good neurosis.

From the moment I prayed out loud in that parking lot, I knew my life had taken a departure from what would be considered "normal" by the Jewish community in which I was raised.

In deference to my Hebrew brethren, and in the interest of full disclosure, I will digress in order to "fill in the gaps" regarding my spiritual background prior to my parking lot prayer on March 5, 1971. * * * * *

My family was a typical Jewish, Midwestern American family. My parents were agnostics. God was never mentioned in our household. They weren't sure there was a God, but they weren't prepared to say there wasn't. They generally made jokes whenever the topic of God came up. The matter was just not relevant for them. What they knew for certain was that we were Jewish.

When I was eight, I began asking my parents questions about God. In response, I received very

> My family was a typical Jewish, Midwestern American family. My parents were agnostics. God was never mentioned in our household.

vague answers. For them, the subject was just not relevant. But I had questions. So, at eight years old, I thought, *'The rabbi's will know the answers to my questions.'*

That was when I asked my parents if I could attend Hebrew school. My father didn't want to spend the money. But, my mother said, *"If he wants to do it, let him. He'll see he won't like it, and he'll quit."* After more discussion, they agreed to enroll me. That's how, at eight years old, I began Hebrew School, which was located at a nearby Orthodox synagogue. Most of my peer group would have given anything to get out of Hebrew school, but I *wanted* to attend. In the beginning, I didn't know a soul, but I liked it anyway.

When I was 10, in the afternoons after Hebrew school, I would frequently get together with my friends. Our home in Chicago was centrally located, so more often than not, they came over to my house. We would regularly discuss philosophical and political topics. We deliberated about the meaning of life, and we considered questions about God. We also had general philosophical discussions, which seemed very natural to me at the time. Although I was usually the initiator of these sessions, my friends clearly found these interchanges stimulating. None of them were ever put off by these talks.

"I wonder if ants realize the brevity of their lives."

"You know, compared to trees, our lives are short. Before we know, we're gonna be old men."

"What is life all about, anyway?" Frequently, it was more philosophical than religious. Looking back, I can see how someone could say, *"What a weird little kid."*

One afternoon, three or four of my friends and I gathered in my bedroom after school. We were in the middle of one of these wide-ranging deliberations when my father walked in. *"What are you guys discussing all the time?"*

I was the spokesman for this particular get-together. Besides, it was *my* father inquiring. *"We were discussing God and His participation in the affairs of men, and the meaning of life. We're wondering to what extent He intervenes in political things or the news."*

After I answered him, my father shrugged his shoulders. I distinctly remember his response. *"Those things are unknowable. Why don't you ask the Pope?"*

That was his way of belittling what we were doing. It didn't stop us, but it's an indication of just how odd this must have appeared to the casual observer.

At the Hebrew school, I felt that I was getting answers. I could ask questions, and they were taken seriously. I would get thoughtful responses to queries about God and the Bible stories. Naturally, I learned how to read Hebrew. We students had no idea what the Hebrew words *meant,* but boy, could we whiz through all those liturgical prayers.

There were girls there too, of course, and we had baseball teams and athletics. I had a social circle at public school, and I had a social circle of synagogue friends. All the other kids hated Hebrew school, but their parents made them attend. Not me. I loved it. I thought it was great. To this day, I recall all the rabbis as very sincere, dedicated men.

At some point, I even insisted the family keep Kosher. I became the knowledgeable Jewish guy of the family. At 10 years old, I was running the annual family Passover Seder.

For five years, I attended Hebrew school five days a week; Monday through Thursday and Sunday school on Sunday. On Saturdays I attended services. Even after my Bar Mitzvah when I turned 13, I continued with the same routine through my first year of high school. This was atypical, as most of my classmates dropped Hebrew School soon after their Bar Mitzvahs.

> I became the knowledgeable Jewish guy of the family. At 10 years old, I was running the annual family Passover Seder.

19—Nice Jewish Boy to Agnostic

After my grandfather, Bernard Liberman, moved to Florida in 1947, I began to spend summers with him and my grandmother Nettie. He was very much like a father to me. I always greatly admired him, and we would just talk and talk and talk. I felt I knew him very well. He always kept a Bible—the Tenach, the Old Testament—by his bed, and he would read it every night.

After I started Hebrew school, I would dialog with my Grandfather on the topics I was learning. Then, I began to ask him pointed questions. *"Grandpa, do you believe the Bible is completely true? Did these things actually happen? What do you think?"* I was in an Orthodox Hebrew school and I respected him, so I asked for his opinion.

"Yes Paul, they happened, but I don't know if they happened just the way the Bible says."

After I entered my sophomore year in high school, it was challenging to attend both high school followed by Hebrew school in the afternoons. Nevertheless, I made the effort until it became too difficult. Plus there was another complicating factor.

When I was 14, I became ill with ulcerative colitis. I also had a friend my age, Steve Winters, who was struggling with the same malady. I was the president of my fraternity at South Shore High School, and Steve was one of my fraternity brothers. He was taking ACTH medicine, and it was blowing him up. I would visit Steve in the hospital, and for a time, it appeared he was going to die. He did eventually survive, but after suffering through years of incapacity.

I was seeing a doctor twice a week for treatments, and taking up to 16 pills a day. I was exhausted all the time from the medical condition, in addition to my busy high school schedule. It was impossible to continue both public school and Hebrew School. This was the reason that led me to finally drop the Hebrew School.

My physical condition was not improving—it was only getting worse. The heavy medications really took away my energy.

I asked the doctor, *"Is this the way it's going to be? Is what's happening to Steve going to happen to me? My father had the same disease, and it was one of the factors that kept him out of the draft. Is this something I'm gonna have to live with all my life?"*

"Well, no Paul. We try to keep it under control with the medication and the treatments. But, I can't promise you anything."

He saw I was very distressed that this was not a temporary thing. He sat down and began to talk to me very personally. *"Paul, I don't know if you can understand, but this is what's called a psychosomatic disease. There's a lot of thought in medical circles that this condition has to do with your emotions. It seems clear to me that, well . . . that you're crying out of your anus. And, that's what's going on."*

I really wanted to understand. *"What do you mean by that?"*

"Paul, it's clear you are very angry, and you've turned it inward on your body. So the idea is, don't turn it in on your body—just let 'er go."

On the way home that day, I started to process what the doctor had said. It didn't take me long to realize I *was* angry!

I was angry at my father.

He wasn't home. He wasn't interested—he didn't care. He didn't know me. He didn't *want* to know me. I felt very much shortchanged. You couldn't get to know him. He didn't want to spend time with me *or* my brothers. It wasn't just me. He had a problem with all of his relationships. Nobody could get beneath the surface with him, and I wanted him to know me better than that. I wanted to know him better, but nothing doing!

I felt shortchanged and very angry about this. But, to be so angry at your father was socially unacceptable. Although I didn't come to that realization right away, that's clearly where the anger was. As I began to let the anger out, it became clear to me with whom I was angry.

And, all along, my mother was cultivating this. As the eldest son, she was taking her dissatisfactions with her husband, my father, and conveying them to me. She didn't do me any favors with this. It was only stoking the flames of anger toward my father. No doubt, there was justification behind her complaints, just as there was behind my complaint. But, seemingly, my father just didn't care.

As I got older, I had more insight on all of this. I realized my mother complained about him most days of the week, but he never complained about her. He probably saw that the home was a hostile place. The four sons and his wife saw him as a bad man. His solution was to go off, and to bury himself in his work and golf. He worked hard in business, and he wanted to enjoy himself with his friends.

The doctor told me, *"Let the anger go. If you'll express your anger, I think your disease will resolve itself. If you don't turn the anger inward but turn it outward."* With that tidbit of information, I felt justified in telling *everyone* off. I soon became a *very* rebellious young man.

By the time I was 16, I was really into this idea of telling people off. I told off my teachers. I would tell off my relatives. If somebody irked me in the store, I'd tell *them* off. Everyone was getting told off by me. Sure enough, within a very short period of time, I no longer had ulcerative colitis. But at the same time, I had become a very vocal, very rebellious, very angry young man.

> Even after Hebrew school, I continued to lay tefillin—the phylacteries—and to read the Hebrew prayers. I continued to say the Shema every morning and every night.

Even after Hebrew school, I continued to lay tefillin—the phylacteries—and to read the Hebrew prayers. I continued to say the Shema every morning and every night. I had all the prayers memorized. Eventually, though, it all began to fade, because I was no longer a part of synagogue life. Gradually, I was no longer afraid to neglect to recite those prayers. At first, there was truly apprehension about not doing them. *'What would God think if I didn't say the prayers?'* I got over that, so that at 16, the synagogue was well behind me.

By the time I was in my 20s, I identified myself as an agnostic. I suppose, I pretty much lined up with my parents thinking on the subject. I wasn't *certain* there wasn't a God, but I had begun to feel it was unknowable one way or the other. At some time, while I was in college, I might have even considered myself an atheist.

After I arrived at the University of Wisconsin, I took a course in comparative

> I wasn't *certain* there wasn't a God, but I had begun to feel it was unknowable one way or the other.

religion which *really* confused the heck out of me and my philosophy. This was the point where I said, *'Maybe there's just no God at all.'*

There were about 30 or 40 students in the class, and it was very intellectual—if not philosophical—in content. The professor was a self-described atheist. He had us read a number of different authors that put forward his perspective. These writers were saying God is totally manmade—that man created God to fulfill mankind's own needs rather than God creating man. Man created God to fill in the gaps for what he didn't understand. Religion became a crutch for the ignorant and the superstitious. We students were certainly getting propagandized. So, during my college years, my thinking was very confused on the subject of God.

An interesting fact was that both of the professor's hands were severely crippled with arthritis. Apparently, a few of the students in my class were born-again Christians. They spoke up; however, I didn't pay much attention to them or to what they were saying. I do remember one of these students proposing, *"You know, it's no accident that your hands are all crippled up. There's a connection between your lack of belief and your crippled-up hands."*

The professor didn't attempt to argue with this. *"I'll grant there might be something out there that is beyond the physical."*

Then he began to talk about ESP and the occult. This was his way of making a concession there might be something—an alternative to his point of view. He was attempting to give equal time as best as he understood what that meant.

The comparative religion course partially accounted for my confusion. In addition, I embraced a hedonistic existence in college. My philosophy basically came down to the proposition, *"If you can get away with it, do it."* Without doubt, it was a very liberal university, and I fit right in.

20—New Jewish Believer

With 20/20 hindsight, it's easy to see that March 5, 1971 was the most significant turning point of my adult life. When I cried out to Jesus, *"I need a Messiah!"* I was aware I had crossed into uncharted territory. My epiphany was that the so-called "New Testament" was, in fact, an extension of the Jewish Bible, the so-called "Old Testament." As I understood in 1971, all Christians, meaning Gentiles, are raised with this truth. As far as I knew, I was the first Jew ever to come to this revelation.

Up until that day, the only New Testament I had been reading was the one at the Library of Congress during my lunch hour and on other occasions when the congressional hearings I attended were on break. I now had many more questions about the Bible and its entire message. This would require a lot of additional reading. My system of running across the street to the Library of Congress wasn't going to work any longer.

I immediately resolved to buy a Bible. So I headed to a local bookstore and asked to be directed to their selection of Bibles. I didn't know one Bible from another. As I looked through the various possibilities, I had a couple of thoughts. *"I don't want to read the King James; that's for the Gentiles."* Also, the Shakespearian English was difficult to read. As I perused the possibilities, I settled on, and bought, a different, modern-English translation. It was easy reading and readily understandable. Previously, the Scriptures had always been so dry, and who was interested in that? But, all of a sudden, with this Bible, I was interested.

It doesn't take long, if you read voraciously, to plow through most of the Bible. I didn't understand all of it, but in rather short order, I did understand enough to cause me to wonder, *'What is this about? Why are there some additional books in this Old Testament? What is this? Why do some Bibles have the book of*

Maccabees and some don't? Why do some have the book of Judith, and some don't? Apparently, there's a difference.'

I was curious, because I recognized a distinction. I couldn't figure out why. It seemed to me these additional books were history, but they didn't have the same ring of truth as the rest of the Bible.

For me, like any typical Jew of my generation, the world was divided into Christians (Gentiles) and Jews. Now that I had embraced the New Testament, I felt this "understanding" brought me into accord with the entire Gentile, Christian population. Any, and all, of them would now be a resource for my new faith. As a result, with my multitude of questions, it was perfectly natural for me to ask my Gentile coworkers for their opinions regarding matters of the New Testament.

It was a revelation to speak to Gentiles about Jesus, the faith, and the Bible, and to discover the majority didn't have a clue what I was talking about. They weren't interested. I was receiving blank stares, the same as the Jewish people with whom I would chat on these topics. They truly didn't want to discuss these matters. At first, I couldn't understand the coolness the inquiries frequently elicited from my associates.

> For me, like any typical Jew of my generation, the world was divided into Christians (Gentiles) and Jews.

But then I discovered other Christians who were right with me and thrilled that I had come into my newly discovered faith. It was a shock when I realized: Not all "Christians" are *Christians*. However, as a result of these random conversations, I began to identify certain of my colleagues who appreciated my inquiries.

I read my new Bible at every extra moment, including at home in the evenings. Of course, Susan saw me reading it. I would comment to her about what I was reading, but received little or no response. She had zero interest.

About a month after I bought my Bible, I asked one of the "friendly" coworkers about the question of the extra books in the Old Testament. *"Paul, let me see your Bible."* I showed him the one I had bought and was now carrying with me. *"See, it's a Catholic Bible. The Catholics have extra books, which are called the Apocrypha. Protestant Bibles do not include these books, nor do they consider them to be the inspired word of God."*

I saw the word *"Catholic"* in my Bible; that was a turn off. But, the English was so *easy* to read. I decided I could continue to use it, especially for the New Testament, but I would give only cursory attention to the *extra* books. I was a brand new believer, but already I seemed to be developing a spiritual radar. I could tell the Bible *alone* was unique in having the ring of truth. I recognized the difference in the "ring of truth," or lack of it, contained in the "extra" books.

That's when I resolved to compare my English-translation Jewish Bible with the Bible I had recently purchased. I especially wanted to match their language with the Messianic prophecies I had studied.

The case for the Messianic predictions was still overwhelming. It paralleled, word for word, 99 and 44/100% the same. In the two places I could find that were questionable, there was some ambiguity in the original Hebrew text. You could make a case either way. It was not conclusively opposed to the Christian Bible—I was satisfied with that. This confirmed to me that I was indeed on the right track—Jesus *was* the Messiah.

After that, I never had any question about the claims of the New Testament, or what it stated about Jesus being God, or anything. I accepted the whole thing. Assuming God wrote this book, whatever is in there—that's the way it is. He says He's God—all right. I had no problem at all with that or anything like that. But, during the first 15-month period, my wife was not with me on this, and I had yet to meet another Jewish believer.

My only bewilderment, *'What do I do with this? Is this just gonna be something that's private, between me and God, and that's it–or what?'* That was a puzzlement for me. That was the center of my struggle. *'What does this mean? What do I do with it?'*

I believed in Providence. I could see clues as to what God wanted me to do and what God was doing, and I should throw in with it. That was the extent of the transaction, as far as I was concerned. After that, I felt I would have God's sponsorship. I was happy to know I was going to go to Heaven, but that's all there was for me. I concluded, that's all this would be.

I recognized I was going to be considered odd by the Jewish community and, in all likelihood, even by my wife. Clearly, there would be no quarter on this matter from my family in Chicago. I assumed I was the first Jew ever to perceive that the New Testament was simply a continuation of the Jewish Bible—that it was actually all one book. I accepted that it would be a lonely road. I concluded that this would have to be something solely between God and me alone. I was apprehensive about that, but if that's what it was, that's what it was.

At the Commerce Department, I continued doing my job, and soon I noticed that people were beginning to speak up for me. *"Liberman? We should keep this guy. Liberman–he does good work."*

Seemingly out of nowhere, people were speaking up for me! *'Hey, maybe it's working.'* My understanding was; my prayer was being answered. That led me to conclude, if God was going to help me out in life, He'd always help me out, and I'd be successful. It was very important to me—to be successful. *'If I'm successful, and I'm tuned in with God, what do I care what anybody says or thinks. The heck with 'em. The heck with 'em.'*

21—The Inquiring Jew

In short order, I plowed through the New Testament. I began to wonder if I had bought into Gentile propaganda. *'You know, Paul, you understand about Judaism, and you've basically read the New Testament, but are you just naïve, Paul? Are you gullible? Maybe you're too easily persuaded into a philosophical fold.'*

That is the moment I set about to investigate and read up on the other major religions of the world. I attempted to approach each one with an open mind. *'Hey, Paul, if Christianity and the New Testament are an extension of Judaism, maybe you'll buy anything. Look at how prejudiced you were against the New Testament.'* That was my logic.

Hinduism

The first religion I investigated was Hinduism. After a time, it struck me that Hinduism had no form or structure. It only had this transmigration from animal to animal, and it was so far out, it appeared to be a product of the imagination with all the freaky-looking monster kinds of things. Not only did Hinduism seem like it was a product of human imagination—it was *the dark side* of the imagination. With all this reincarnation and transmigration going on, I wondered, *'Who's up there directing traffic? "You're gonna be an insect. You're gonna be a brahma bull."'*

Buddhism

After that, I got the idea that Buddhism was a reformed version of Hinduism which turned out to be accurate. Buddhism disposed of the particular feature of the transmigration. But, it had no stated ideal. Buddhism is about doing a head job on yourself to relax your mind; the way to find out about a whole lot of things is simply to get your mind relaxed. *"You gotta get your mind relaxed so that you'll know."* You said your mantra, you relaxed the mind, you stared at a candle (or whatever it was), to relax the mind. Get your brain waves down, and you'll *know* things. The focus was on the relaxation of the mind; and through the relaxation of the mind, you would "come into contact" with knowing things. It reminded me of something I participated in that had to do with bio-feedback. *'This is the same thing as Silva Mind Control.'* Mind control is the same thing—relax the mind.

That led me to think, *'That's the same thing the Bible says. "Be still and know." The Bible, though, has a complete comprehensive philosophy—this does not. This just has a thing where you're reincarnated. If you're reincarnated endlessly, then there is no Heaven and Hell—there's no right and wrong.'*

Buddhism didn't appear to have much of a morality to it. It was an abstraction of morality. It didn't sound right to me that there was nothing to give me any assurance of where I stood in the universe. There was no way to know. How would you know that what you knew was correct? How would you *know* that you *knew?*

It didn't have any substance to it. I decided, *'This really doesn't structure my universe very well.'* I was looking for answers, and Buddhism didn't offer any. It was all too nebulous.

Hare Krishna

Reading about Hinduism and Buddhism led me to the Hare Krishna version of Eastern religion. In 1971, Hare Krishna was high profile. They were out on the city streets very publicly dancing with their bald heads, and their orange garments and tambourines, jumping up and down. So, I would engage them and ask a lot of questions.

Their thing was to sing for hours upon hours. In the singing, and in the self-deprivation, they would enter into a semi-trance as yet another means of knowing—a variation of the Buddhist and Hindu Eastern religion. Hare Krishna had to do with self-mortification—intentionally making yourself a reproach in society, and singing or chanting in an effort to lose yourself in the process—to lose your sense of self-awareness—in order that you would go into a trance and thereby obtain *knowing*. This was what I came to understand about it.

I attempted to visualize myself doing this. *'As a Jew, I believe that Abraham, Isaac, and Jacob existed. I don't believe that's what they had to do to get in touch with God. So, it isn't necessary, and therefore, why do it? What's the point?'* I dismissed it, and that's the reason I dismissed it.

'All right, the Bible says, "Be still and know." I can do that without getting into all this hokey Eastern stuff.'

Islam

I read up on *everything*, which brought me to Islam. It was initially presented to me as an extension of Judaism and Christianity.

I made another trip to the Library of Congress to read the Koran. It seemed to me that Muhammad was a tribal leader and a political leader who was responsible for coalescing the various tribal peoples. Right from the beginning, he saw the one-god concept as valid. In Arabia, during his time, they all had separate gods. Muhammad was saying, *"No, there's only one god."*

At the beginning, he spoke very respectfully of the people of the book—the Jewish people—and the Bible. In reading the Koran, I noticed a progression—his attitude changed. Muhammad wanted the Jewish people to agree that he would be "the one" for the Arabs. The Koran would be the revelation for the Arabic peoples. But, he was also attempting to be endorsed and embraced by the Jewish people. When the Jewish people did not embrace him, or his revelations, he turned on them. The revision of attitude occurred during the time between his ministry in Mecca and Medina. When the Jewish establishment would not embrace him, he began to oppose the Jews.

The sentiment of the Koran seemed to be very contradictory to the Bible. For example, the New Testament talks about God having a Son. In Islam, to say this is considered blasphemy. It can't be both ways. It is either one or the other.

I really couldn't pick up the philosophical thread of Islam, although I actually tried. Something else bothered me—a lot. The order of events in Muhammad's telling was out of sync with the Bible. For example: Moses and Jesus and David. The Bible provides a very definite chronology of the biblical characters— who came first. That commonly accepted history is completely jumbled in Islam. So, how could this possibly be simply an extension of Judaism and Christianity?

The Koran was really, really boring. I found myself skimming the pages because it was *so* terribly tedious. The sentences were dreadfully long. It purported to add to the Bible—the *"new revelation"*—but, it was totally inconsistent with the Bible.

I remembered all the Bible stories from my training in Hebrew school, and I had read the New Testament. The Koran was very inconsistent with the Bible, and I was aware of the inconsistency. *'How could this be an extension or addition to the Bible, if it's so much at variance with the Bible? That can't be! God is not confused, and He doesn't contradict Himself.'*

I felt as if I owed it to myself to be able to honestly state that I had thoughtfully considered Islam. That led me to read the second book, the Hadith, which is a commentary on the Koran. But, I had no appetite for it, either. The Hadith turned out to be even more boring than the Koran. I gave it only a surface perusal. At some point, you realize you're simply fulfilling an obligation to yourself, and you start skimming.

Early on, Islam seemed like a bunch of hokum to me. Also, it didn't give me the loving, mellow feeling. I always received a really mellow feeling when reading the Bible, and particularly while reading the New Testament. Studying the other religions was not mellow. Reading the Koran was upsetting and disturbing. I dismissed Islam pretty much out of hand because, I soon realized, I didn't want to read it. It just didn't bear pursuing. I was looking for *"it,"* whatever *"it"* was.

Also, Islam made no serious effort at prophecy. That was a major issue for me. It did *not* have prophecy. *None of these other world religions contained specific, fulfilled prophecy.* As soon as I realized these alternative religions didn't have prophecy, they were off the table for serious consideration. The validity of prophecy could not be denied. In Hinduism, Buddhism, Hare Krishna, and Islam, there was *no prophecy anywhere in sight.* For me, that undermined their credibility more than any other issue.

The more I read about the other religions, the more I became convinced that the Bible was it. Instead of undermining my faith, all this wide-ranging

> *None of these other world religions contained specific, fulfilled prophecy.* As soon as I realized these alternative religions didn't have prophecy, they were off the table for serious consideration.

investigation was confirming my faith. I had made my decision, but I wanted to reassure myself I hadn't simply bought into some sort of Gentile propaganda.

Christian Science

After this, on my lunch hours, I began to visit a Christian Science reading room located in a storefront close to where I worked. I stopped in to investigate.

My conclusion: Christian Science didn't seem like it was a love relationship with a person. It was all very abstract, cold, and impersonal. It was a science—Christian *"Science."* They maintain there is a connection between faith and healing, but their system has nothing to do with a relationship. Love was not the issue for Christian Science. On the other hand, the New Testament was very personal. I discovered nothing cold and abstract about the New Testament. Far from it, the New Testament was full of pathos. Christian Science just didn't have that pathos for me. Quite the opposite. I concluded Christian Science was not worth considering further.

Moonies

At some point, I investigated the Moonies. This was the Unification Church, founded and led by Sun Myung Moon. They were popular at the time, especially in Washington, DC. It was in the atmosphere of the 70s.

The Moonies bought newspapers and other business enterprises. I never gave that point particular credibility. I wanted to find out what they were saying about the Reverend Sun Moon. It seemed that he implied he was the messiah. He never overtly stated as much, but he *implied* it. The importance of world events and the spread of faith in Korea was a large part of their worldview. To me, it seemed more reasonable that *Israel* was the important place and should be the focus. *'Wait a minute. Israel is the place — not Korea. Come on!'*

The Moonie religion was also very inconsistent with the Bible. When I understood they were implying the Reverend Moon was the messiah, I began to think, *'We already have a Messiah. What are they saying—that he is another messiah? Or, are they saying he's the second coming of the Messiah?*

'If they're saying we have another messiah, that can't be right. The Bible doesn't speak about there being two messiahs. Or, if he's the second coming of the Messiah, Sun Moon is not coming the way the Bible says the Messiah is coming back.' For me, the Moonie religion was easily dismissible.

Continued Bible Reading—But No Church

At the same time as I was on my quest to read up on, and to examine, the other major world religions, I diligently continued to read the New Testament. I never let up on that, and was reading quite a lot of the Bible. I had also gotten back into the Old Testament. In the beginning, I read the Gospels. I read one and then moved on to some of the other texts in the New Testament. I didn't understand much at the beginning, but I was very interested in it. Then, I went back and began to read, as well, from the Old Testament.

One thing I did *not* do was visit a church. That was for Gentiles. I was a Jewish guy. How obvious: *Jewish people don't go to church*. It was not even on the radar. I wouldn't step foot in a church. It was unthinkable—out of the question. That left me very much on my own: my own search, my own investigation, my own journey. As far as I knew, I was the first Jew in 2,000 years to come to the conclusion that the New Testament is a valid extension of the Bible and Jesus is the Messiah of the *Jews*—and not just the *Gentiles'* Messiah. I wasn't sure exactly how to proceed, but it was a given for me that church wasn't an option.

At the same time, I was having a lot of conversations with people. As I examined one of these other religious possibilities, I talked to people. As I was reading, I was asking questions. I was constantly in conversations. I asked other people what they thought and solicited feedback.

> One thing I did *not* do was visit a church. That was for Gentiles. I was a Jewish guy. How obvious: *Jewish people don't go to church.*

If I went to a Christian Science Reading Room, I took that opportunity to be involved in a conversation. I was in an ongoing dialog with a guy at the Commerce Department about Mormonism. As I was looking into these different religions, I would ask questions. I would see Hare Krishnas on the street, and I would go up and engage them. *"What are you guys all about?"* I was asking a lot of questions. The investigation of other religions largely had to do with reassuring myself that I was correct. The more I read up on the other religions and talked to people, the more reassured I was. *'The world doesn't understand, but boy, I have this right!'*

Are There Others Like Me?

This period of investigation went on for 15 months, beginning right after my parking lot prayer. Toward the end of the 15 months, I was going through the telephone book, and I saw an advertisement in the yellow pages for the American Board of Missions to the Jews. That struck me as curious, so I took down their address in Washington, DC and set off to visit them. I wanted to find out what this was all about because I didn't know any other Jewish believers.

I pulled into the driveway, but before I could go to the door, I saw a car in the driveway. It had a bumper sticker that really caught my attention: *Jews for Jesus*. I sat there and looked at it for a good five minutes, staring at it, wondering, *'What does this mean?'* I kept turning over in my mind, *'What could this mean?'* I hadn't a glimmer of an idea.

After sitting for a while pondering that bumper sticker, I went to the front door of the house and rang the doorbell. A woman answered and I immediately began to quiz her; *"What is this place? What is American Board of Missions to the Jews? What does that mean?"* She was cautious about telling me who and what she was. She wanted to know who and what *I* was all about. Eventually, we broke the ice, and she invited me in.

After we were seated in her living room, she introduced herself as Mrs. Miller. She and her husband, Bob, were the directors of the Washington, DC chapter of the American Board of Missions to the Jews. I told her my name was Paul Liberman and explained to her that I was a Jew who now accepted the New Testament as valid. Therefore, I believed that Jesus is the Messiah. I explained that I had never met another Jewish believer and was really curious about the name of their organization.

Mrs. Miller shared the history of the organization (which, in 1988, became known as "Chosen People Ministries"). The founder, Leopold Cohn, was born in Berezna, a small town and Orthodox Jewish community in eastern Hungary. He studied and became Rabbi Cohn. During his rabbinic studies, Rabbi Cohn became obsessed with questions about the Messiah. He was unable to get satisfactory answers to his questions from local resources. Oddly enough, he was advised to travel to America where *they know more about the Messiah."* His inquiries led him to be absolutely persuaded that Jesus was, in fact, the Messiah. In 1894, Leopold Cohn founded the American Board of Missions to the Jews in the Brownsville section of Brooklyn, New York.

I found all of this quite amazing, but I told her I still hadn't yet met any Jewish believers. Mrs. Miller assured me there were, indeed, others. After we visited awhile, she invited me to come back. I thanked her for her kindness and left.

This certainly was a potential shift in my thinking. *'Are there really others out there like me?'*

22—My Mormon Supervisor

During my initial trip to Washington, DC, Dr. Robert Miller, who was the Director for the Office of Domestic Business Policy, originally interviewed me at the Commerce Department. He hired me for a job in that department, but just a month after I started to work, he was let go.

My second job assignment at the Commerce Department had me writing opinions regarding proposed business legislation on behalf of the Nixon administration. My supervisor for this position happened to be a Mormon.

Ordinarily, that factoid would not even come up for discussion except that after my decision to embrace the New Testament, my own behavior began to evolve. My jargon was beginning to take on shades of the New Testament and some remark he picked up on alerted him that I was now a believer. So, we had that in common—we could both talk about the New Testament. That's also when he first identified me as a potential candidate for the Mormon Church, and thus the recruitment began.

I was uncomfortable with the dialogue from the beginning. It was *not* by my initiative. The conversations were instigated by him and his own sense of mission. I was completely disinterested in any wide-ranging discussion on the topic of Mormonism.

I was very open with anyone who would listen that something monumental had occurred in my life. I was regularly having random conversations with all kinds of people. New believers are very zealous. I was taking every opportunity to strike up a conversation on various topics. I don't recall how the subject originally was broached; whether by him or me, or what was even said, but it turned to Mormon beliefs. Almost instantly, there was pressure from him, and I became very uncomfortable. Next, he gave me a *Book of Mormon* and offered details regarding Joseph Smith.

I took home the *Book of Mormon* and I didn't just skim it; I actually read it. That only seemed to encourage him. At every opportunity, he wanted to bring up the subject. He would ask pointed questions about my reading.

It wasn't long before he passed on my name to his Mormon colleagues, and they began to come around to the house. I was already having difficulties with Susan who first saw her Jewish husband reading the booklet about Bible prophecy, then the New Testament, and now, the Book of Mormon! She put up a wall whenever I attempted to discuss "the subject" with her. Now, we had Mormons coming to our house, and they wanted to show us movies about Joseph Smith and the Mormon Church while they pointed out different things about good King Darius.

Mormons have a special doctrine for Jewish people. Jews will all be in Heaven, second in the hierarchy only under the Mormons because the stick of Judah and the stick of Ephraim will come together. They believe Mormons are derived from the stick of Ephraim. That's what I read in the Book of Mormon. If a Jew becomes a Mormon, he is now first in Heaven with the other Mormons, and no longer second. Blacks can also get into the kingdom of Heaven. They'll be slaves forever, but at least they will be in Heaven. That didn't sound right to me. The whole notion seemed wrong.

There were other peculiar ideas. For example, during the three days until the resurrection, Jesus was off in the United States and was married with wives. Three Nephites (a people spoken of in the Book of Mormon) still roam the Earth from the time of Jesus' visit to the America's; blessed by Him not to experience death until His Second Coming. The Garden of Eden was located in Missouri at the time Adam and Eve were kicked out. Native Americans are the descendants of the Lamanites—another people spoken of in the Book of Mormon. There were so many far out things. The more they talked, the more I was not sold. The more they told me, the more I was sure *this wasn't it.*

Up to this point, Susan was not buying any of it; not the New Testament and certainly not Mormonism. For her, it was *all* equally weird. But, she had to listen because my job was on the line. I cautioned her that we had to go easy because I was only a day-to-day consultant. Every single day, I was required to ask my Mormon supervisor for permission to return to work the next day. Susan and I both did our best to be gracious—what choice did we have? We listened, and we were polite.

I didn't want to offend my boss, but the more I read and heard on the subject of Mormonism, the more it appeared to be *mishegas*–craziness. However, I didn't want to argue with him; it was not in my best interest.

The main thing that convinced me Mormonism was untrue had to do with prophecy. That was the

> The more I read and heard on the subject of Mormonism, the more it appeared to be *mishegas*–craziness.

key element for me—prophecy. The Book of Mormon *has* prophecy, but it's *a different kind* of prophecy. It has to do with Joseph Smith. In the early 1800s, he wrote down history that dated back to 600 years BCE. That prophecy then was proclaimed to have come true.

That caused me to consider, *'Whoa, whoa, wait a minute! That's not venturing out into the future. That's reporting back that somebody made prophecy predicting the future. That could still be 20/20 hindsight by someone in the 19th century.'*

There were all of these extraordinary ideas that were so difficult to swallow, I just couldn't see it for beans. At work, I restrained my skepticism on the Mormon subject because he was my superior. I knew he was testing my faith, and I was aware I dared not offend the man. But, I also couldn't allow him to believe I agreed with him.

At a certain point, I needed for him to get off my case. I didn't want them coming to the house anymore. Eventually, I told him, *"Don't send anyone else. My wife already thinks that I've gone off the deep end. I can't have anyone coming to the house anymore. You've asked me to consider this. I have considered it, but I'm having problems with it."*

"What exactly are your problems, Paul?"

I explicitly told him my issues. *"I can accept the New Testament, which we both accept. But, this Mormon thing, the more I* read about it—the more it seems to me the author is consciously imitating the tone of the Scriptures. The Book of Mormon doesn't have the same feel to it that it is the same writer as those in the Bible. The language of the Book of Mormon is, 'And, so-and-so did such-and-such exceedingly,' and then something else 'exceedingly,' and then something else 'exceedingly.' It bothers me that this word 'exceedingly' is always coming up, and I don't see that in the Old or New Testaments.*

"It has a different ring to it. The Book of Mormon just doesn't have that ring of truth, and it doesn't have prophecy in the way I understand how prophecy is supposed to venture out into the future."

> "Don't send anybody else. My wife already thinks that I've gone off the deep end. I can't have anyone coming to the house anymore."

He was a very patient guy—and very sincere. At one time, he was a Mormon missionary in South America, and he was eager to spread the faith. He was always very respectful to me. As it turned out, he didn't get upset that I wasn't buying into it, and he graciously let me off the hook. Fortunately, I was reassigned and was no longer his subordinate. It worked out, but the Mormon period went on for a few months, until I was finally reassigned. That took care of the problem.

23—Meeting at the White House

I began work at the Commerce Department in February 1971. I had just turned 29, and I was a per diem (day-to-day) consultant. I was given an assignment designator, and was working as a legislative analyst writing the Commerce Department's opinion on various pieces of business legislation. This entailed making regular trips up to Capitol Hill and sitting in on the hearings. Things appeared to be panning out. February went by and then March. But, I was still not a regular employee. April went by, and then May, and yet nothing really changed regarding my status, so I decided to relax a bit. I took comfort that at least I was getting paid.

That's when someone tipped me off that Dave Lambert didn't want me. Dave was the new department head who replaced Robert Miller—the man who originally hired me for the Commerce Department. The word was, *"Dave Lambert wants to put his own man in there."*

Once this fact became clear to me—that the new guy planned to get rid of me—I was rattled. What was I going to do? I was vulnerable. I might as well have a target on my back or a sign that read, "Temporary."

One afternoon, I was hanging out at the new Republican Club, which was my routine. I had taken out a lifetime membership at the Capitol Hill Club when they moved to their new building located one block from the United States Capitol. A lot of drinking went on there, as well as a lot of networking. Various trade-association representatives, also regulars, would talk to me because they wanted influence with someone in the Commerce Department. That particular day, I was speaking with a guy who headed up the National Insurance Trade Association. We were becoming quite chummy, as we had previously visited on several occasions. On this particular day, when he asked me what was happening in my life, I began to fill him in on my tenuous situation at Commerce.

"Paul, I happen to know you raised a good deal of money for Senator Paul Fannin of Arizona. Are you aware I used to be the administrative assistant for Senator Fannin? Paul, you've raised money for Republicans all over the country. Why don't you call in some of your chits? Think about it. These people are here in Washington, DC. Charlie Barr is in Chicago. You should be able to do this for yourself. You don't have to ask Charlie, 'Mother may I?' Just get busy and reach out to some of these contacts! Listen, I'm going to call Senator Fannin's new administrative assistant and tell him, 'Hey, Paul's in trouble.' Charlie is backing you on this, right?"

"Oh, sure! Absolutely!"

Right away, the Commerce Department started getting calls from all over Capitol Hill! Messages were coming in about this guy, Liberman, who can't get

> *Paul, you've raised money for Republicans all over the country. Why don't you call in some of your chits?*

his employment paperwork through the bureaucracy! *"Hey, this fellow worked for us and he raised a lot of money for us! He's in trouble, and he's Charlie's man!"* This really stirred things up! Now I was at war with the Commerce Department. At the same time, I was doing everything to fight off Dave Lambert who was attempting to fire me. I continued to escalate the matter until finally, I told him, *"I want to appeal to your superior and to his superior in the bureaucracy."*

That was my strategy. I was prolonging the matter while this squabble was going on—delaying, and appealing, and hoping for a break. It was the right decision—to start calling in chits—as there started to be a shift in the momentum. I worked my way up the ladder at the Commerce Department with the issue. Eventually, I was appealing my case in the office of the assistant to the Secretary of Commerce. *"Well Paul, I want you to know we've really tried to work this out, but Dave Lambert wants his own guy and it's his call."*

"Then I need to appeal this." That was what I had been doing—buying myself more time at $100 a day—appealing and delaying.

"Paul, there is no other place left to appeal except to the White House."

"Then that's what I want to do. I want to appeal my case to the White House—to the Republican Party I have worked for. As you're aware, I did good work, and the Republican Party should be able to keep its commitment to me. I quit my job in Chicago and sold my house. I moved my family here to Washington, DC based on the promise of a job. I want to talk to someone at the White House."

I was actually stalling again in another effort to buy time. However, the next thing I know, the Commerce Department made an appointment for me at the White House. Now they were done with me. No one else at Commerce had to deal with me. It was someone else's problem.

> *"I want to appeal my case to the White House—to the Republican Party I have worked for."*

That evening when I called Charlie Barr, I told him about the appointment at the White House. *"Which day? I'm coming to that meeting. I am going with you to the White House."*

The meeting was set for July 14. Charlie and I headed over to the White House where we met with Fred Malek, who was the director of personnel at the Nixon White House. It was my meeting, so I laid out my case, explaining the entire situation up to the present day. Charlie was sitting back, quietly listening, attentive to everything being said. At some point, Fred Malek turned toward Charlie and interjected. *"You didn't introduce me to your friend."*

"I'm sorry," I apologized. *"This is Charles Barr. He's an attorney and he requested that he join me for this meeting."*

"I know who Charlie Barr is."

Charlie had previously told me he had never met Fred Malek, so I was a bit surprised. *"Really?"*

"Oh, yeah. I know who Charlie Barr is. Charlie Barr doesn't know it, but he gave me my career."

Charlie was quietly sitting there, taking in our conversation. This was the director of personnel at the Nixon White House stating it was Charlie Barr who was responsible for his career! Addressing Charlie directly, he continued. *"Charlie, Congressman Buz Lukens of Ohio was your protégé. You put him into Congress. He was my mentor. That's how I'm in this office."* Then he turned back to me. *"Okay Paul. We'll see to this. We're going to take care of this matter."*

As we were leaving the White House, Charlie proffered, *"Paul, you are a whole lot better off now than you were two hours ago. Now you have the director of White House personnel making calls on your behalf."* Leaving that meeting, I was walking on air. I remember thinking, *'It's in the bag.'*

24—White House Conference

September rolled around, but nothing happened to improve my job status following the July meeting at the White House. The Commerce Department was contacted, but even though the call was from the White House, nobody budged. One afternoon, I was discussing all this with a colleague when he set me straight. *"Paul, don't you know what's going on? You can only legally be a per-diem employee for one year. You're distressed about how long it's taking for there to be some word about something; but can't you see they're just delaying, waiting for the clock to run out? You're a per-diem consultant. In your case, about eight months of this time is used up. They're trying to wait you out. They're stalling to try and get rid of you altogether."*

This really lit a fire under me, so I contacted Fred Malek at the White House. *"I'm trying to be patient, but it was July 14th when I met with you and this is now September."*

Actually, I was so frustrated by this point, I just blew up. *"What the heck? You made all these nice-sounding promises with Charlie Barr there. You're supposed to be with the Republican Party. I worked years for the Republican Party. I moved here to Washington, DC from Chicago, and I've been doing good work with the assignments I've been given. What about all this? Does it all count for nothing? Does no one care?*

"After all this time I'm still just a day-to-day per diem consultant. I still don't have the permanent position I was originally promised. I'm now aware that there's a law; a person cannot hold the classification of a per-diem consultant for more than one full year. They're attempting to run out the clock on us. They're stalling us and trying to pull the wool over our eyes. You should be upset as well, because they are not dealing in a straightforward fashion with you, either."

I blew my cork at him. I told him off! Even though this was the Director of Personnel at the White House, out of frustration, I really let loose at him. *"Well, Paul, I guess I need to get back into this."* He had set it aside. The Commerce Department said they were going to take care of it. In fact, they had done nothing. So now, Fred Malek called an Assistant Secretary in the Commerce Department.

"What's going on over there? I called you before on this Liberman matter, and I thought we had an understanding. It's come to my attention that nothing at all has been done to resolve this!" Now, he blows his temper at the Assistant Secretary of Commerce. Malek got very upset because he now understood they were trying to outmaneuver him. He gave them a dish of what I had given to him.

Now the Commerce Department *really* has a fire going. Their own people are saying I am doing good work, and they should keep me around. Senators and congressmen have called to speak up on my behalf, and the White House is lobbying for me. There was a tug of war going on, and not a new one for the nation's capital. It was the tug between the two sides of government—the political side and the bureaucratic side.

A few days later, I was invited to the office of the same Assistant Secretary of Commerce. He told me he finally recognized what had been taking place. *"Paul, I received a call from the White House. I've investigated your situation. The guy who's trying to get rid of you—let's just say it's very much to your credit that he has it in for you, because we've got it in for him. He's really failed us. He's gone on a liquor bender and left his wife. He even disappeared and left his car in the parking lot with a flat tire. It's been here for a month, and we can't even find the guy. The fact that he wanted to get rid of you stands to your credit."*

"If you want the job that was originally offered to you, you can have it. But, Paul, I'm not sure that is necessarily the best thing

for you. The Office of Domestic Business Policy is about to have a reduction in force. With you being the newest employee, you would most certainly be caught in that RIF (Reduction in Force.) So, I'll give you the job that was originally supposed to be yours; but it's no good, because you're going to be swept up in the RIF.

"Paul, you've been unfairly dealt with on this, but I have a potential solution. It could be a win-win for everyone.

"Some time ago, Maurice Stans (Secretary of Commerce), was charged with putting on an event, "White House Conference—the Industrial World Ahead—A Look at Business in 1990*" However, this has never gotten off the ground. This is going to be very embarrassing for the Secretary.*

"I understand that when you first arrived, you were the one who drew up the outline for this conference. Since that time, they have been following your outline for putting it on. However, it just isn't happening, and we're running short on time. What I want to do, Paul, is assign you to the group that's working on this conference. I want you to go in there and do what you can to energize things. President Nixon is expecting a conference. This is going to be very embarrassing for Secretary Stans if it doesn't come off well.

"I know you were originally hired by Robert Miller. He was relieved of his policy duties at the Office of Domestic Policy, but he is still responsible for putting on this conference. We have less than 90 days, and it hasn't gotten off the ground. Paul, right now you're a per-diem consultant. I'm sure you're aware there is a one-year legal time limitation for that status. In your case, about eight months is used up. If you can turn this thing around and make it all happen—I assure you, I'll personally see to it that you get a really good reward—a permanent position in the Commerce Department. No matter what, just make it happen."

I accepted the assignment without hesitation. It appeared to be the most direct route to resolving my tenuous work status. This solution also had the additional benefit of bringing me out from under the authority of my Mormon supervisor. Once again my direct supervisor was Robert Miller, the man who first hired me when I came to Washington, DC with Charlie Barr. Even though he had been fired, he had agreed to continue with the conference.

The Commerce Department had painted themselves into a corner. They were obligated to the White House to produce a conference by January 1972, and there was less than 90 days to make it happen.

> **Bureaucracy does not handsomely reward initiative or results. But it can be brutal in punishing mistakes or failures.**

I went to work and thoroughly applied myself. Amazingly, the entire thing came together in short order. People had been working on this project for months. They just needed a more aggressive campaign style—not a bureaucratic style. I completely threw myself into making the conference happen. That's what I'd been asked to do.

Robert Miller was the titular head—the senior guy with the Ph.D. He had all the credentials, but I had the outline. I was the assistant, but he was in charge of it. My part was to provide the dynamic energy, and that's what I attempted to do. I was like a foreman of the operation.

There has always been a historic tension in government. The tension is between politics and bureaucracy. Early on, there was a slogan I was required to learn while working for Charlie Barr—*"Get it done or get it right!"* Bureaucracy does not handsomely reward initiative or results. But it can be brutal in punishing mistakes or failures. In government, careers are not made as often by succeeding as by staying out of trouble–not messing up. The emphasis is on *getting it right!*

24—White House Conference

When I was assigned to the White House Conference group, people were operating more like bureaucrats. No one wanted to make a move without some group leader or supervisor approving it first. Like bureaucrats, they were more afraid of making a mistake than getting things done. They were trying to *get it right!* My goal was to operate more as if it was a campaign. I was a political guy. I'd come in off the campaign trails. Drawing on my past experience, I instilled the *"get it done"* mantra. *"Don't wait for approval. Unless you've got a real concern, don't ask, just get it done!"*

I made sure the presidents and CEOs of the nation's largest corporations and businesses were personally contacted and invited to attend the White House Conference. Also invited were the heads of the nation's largest labor unions. President Nixon's cabinet members, who were pertinent to industry, also received special invitations.

There were two dozen people working on this thing. In short order, it all fell into place very nicely. My timing was opportune. People had been working on this for many months before I arrived. However, once I got in there, it did all seem to click. I felt like, *'Gee, I just happened to show up at exactly the right time and everything came together.'* I applied myself, but so had the other people. I don't know that I did anything so extraordinary, but the timing was there. In any case, people seemed to think I had really done something special. In fact, it was the product of a lot of people working together. The end result was that we had our White House conference, and it turned out to be a fantastic success.

It was held at the Shoreham Hotel in central Washington, DC. We had several outstanding speakers including President Nixon. The theme of the Conference—*The Industrial World Ahead: A Look at Business in 1990*—was very forward thinking; but, at a time when the nation was attempting to put the Vietnam War behind, it resonated to be projecting an economic future for a peace-time economy.

24—White House Conference

The conference was a one-week event. It was well attended. President Nixon showed up on occasion. A speech he gave one evening was really outstanding. He was not a formidable speaker; but this conference was supposed to be visionary regarding the economy, and he was quite believable. Everyone could see that he really wanted good things for the economy and for business and it came across in his speaking.

While the conference was underway, I was a functionary. I was making things hum, making sure proceedings went off on schedule and without a hitch. So, I was running around at this conference, putting out "fires," when abruptly someone grabbed my arm and swung me around. It was the Assistant Secretary of Commerce who had appealed to me, as a personal favor to him, to take on the White House Conference.

He pulled me into a corner. *"Paul, you have really done it! This is a tremendous success. I don't know how you did it, but I'm going to keep my word to you. I couldn't have asked for it to be any better. This is a real credit to the entire department. Monday, I'm going to be looking around for the right job for you. You're going to have a permanent position in the Commerce Department. I'm personally going to see to it. I'll be in touch next week. You are going to be very happy with these developments."*

That evening as I was driving home; I was lost in thought. *'Will you look at this? God is actually working on my behalf!'* From that moment, I began to use the term, *"The guiding hand of Providence."* From that time until today, Providence has always played a very key place in my thinking. For me, it's not subjective—some kind of a touchy-feely thing. Providence is objective evidence that God is real.

25—Going After the Bureaucracy

One evening, near the conclusion of the White House Conference, in a private moment, the Assistant Secretary of the Commerce Department pulled me aside. It seems he attributed to me significant credit for the successful event.

When the next week rolled around, I received a call to come to the office of the Assistant Secretary. *"Paul, I have located five vacancies in the Commerce Department that would fit you. All of them are at, or above, $28,000; a pay grade comparable to what you're already making as a per-diem consultant. I am personally making appointments for you with the various department heads where the jobs are located. I want you to look all of them over, but I think I know the one that fits you the best—the one that would really work with what you have shown you are capable of. There's something currently underway here at the Commerce Department which would be especially suited to you."*

Obviously, my expectations were elevated, but as I began to make the rounds to interview, no one was really thinking I was hot stuff. *"What kind of credentials do you have other than political? What do you really know about operating in government—having worked solely in the electrical business?"*

One afternoon, I showed up for an interview with a gentleman by the name of Joe Wright. He was the administrator of a brand new organization only recently formed that was identified as The Social and Economic Statistics Administration (SESA). I was there for a yet-to-be-filled position—Assistant to the Administrator. The job would entail my working directly for Joe Wright, my interviewer.

As he related it to me, *SESA* was created as an oversight organization that then contained two bureaus key to the development of the economic statistics generated by the federal government. One was the Census Bureau, and the other was the

Bureau of Economic Analysis. The Census Bureau had tens of thousands of employees. The Bureau of Economic Analysis had only 600 employees.

> *"Paul, I believe that you're a capable fellow. However, there are a lot of capable people in Washington, DC.*

The Census Bureau develops most of the statistics that are used in the formulation of the Gross National Product, the Balance of Payments, and all the myriad reports that are publically released.

The Bureau of Economic Analysis gets most of its data from the Census Bureau surveys. There are 600 such surveys going on at any one moment in time within the Census Bureau. The Bureau of Economic Analysis also gathers data from the Bureau of Labor Statistics, the Federal Reserve, and other agencies scattered throughout the federal government. The Bureau of Economic Analysis would massage the numbers and then release the publicly reported data that regularly appears in the press.

After we covered the basics of the interview, Mr. Wright looked at me with a deeply penetrating stare that kind of made me shutter, (although I doubt he was aware of it). *"Paul, let me be frank with you. I believe that you're a capable fellow. However, there are a lot of capable people in Washington, DC. Nevertheless, you do have an outstanding and truly distinctive attribute—one that is readily apparent and clearly shows up in your political background. You're not afraid of high-level people—important people. You are used to dealing with them, and you're not intimidated. This is what I see in you, and it is extremely desirable for this particular job."* As I'm listening to him, I'm thinking to myself, *'He thinks I'm not easily intimidated by men in places of power, but something about this guy is scary.'* There was a coldness–a remoteness–to his demeanor. I couldn't put my finger on it.

25—Going After the Bureaucracy

"In fact, Paul, it is an essential requirement. In this job, you will have to go into people's offices and find out how certain numbers and statistics are formulated. The information we're after does not appear in print anywhere, and the Nixon Administration wants to know how these figures are generated. These numbers are critical to the success of the Administration's economic plans.

"How are they gathered? From whom are they gathered? It's just not published anywhere and Paul, we need to uncover it. I assure you, there's going to be resistance. You will have to confront people in order to get it out of them, and they're not going to willingly provide it to you.

"This is an election year and the Nixon administration feels the bureaucrats generating the numbers are skewing this data which, in turn, affects things politically. Civil servants tend to be Democrats. In Washington, DC we're all aware that 80% of bureaucrats are Democrats, and the Administration is suspicious that critical numbers are being massaged to keep the Administration from looking good. It's the reason our organization was formed—to oversee and more or less manage these two bureaus which are responsible for the nation's economic statistics.

"President Nixon has come to the conclusion the bureaucrats are cooking the books on the figures released, especially the GNP (Gross National Product), the Balance of Payments, and others. The President has asked, 'How do I trust these numbers? My fate is in the hands of the bureaucrats, and we don't even know how they formulate these numbers.' There are vested interests who don't want the scrutiny. They believe this information is their private province, and they certainly don't want individuals they perceive to be 'politicians' delving into their machinations.

"Within the Census Bureau, we have many, many divisions, and each division has its field of study. You, Paul, will go in there and analyze each program. Not only will you find out what it is they do, but you also need to find out how they do it to formulate their particular piece of the statistical puzzle.

"There are vested interests who don't want the scrutiny. They believe this information is their private province."

"Also, we believe there's a lot of fat in the number of people we employ in the Census Bureau. While you're looking into each division, we'd also like you to tell us where you think the fat can be cut. You will almost certainly be resisted when you attempt to discover this information. Every resource and tactic will be used to stonewall, but you've got to get to the bottom of this. Some heads are going to have to roll, and they'll see you coming. You will have to be fearless. The Administration needs this information. I'm counting on you to do that. You won't make a lot of friends, but Paul, I'll be backing you up. This Department will be backing you up."

There was nothing to think about. I knew he was right. This was an opportunity I was completely suited for. It ended the uncertainty of my job situation, which had been lingering since I'd first arrived in Washington, DC. I started on February 2, 1972, right after I turned 30. I was now officially employed as a "civil servant." This was almost one year to the day after I had originally started as a per-diem consultant for the Commerce Department.

During the next couple of years, I did what I had been asked to do. As the Assistant to the Administrator for SESA, I ferreted out, and sometimes filched, the different items that went into the statistics the federal government was releasing. The published numbers have a major impact on how the public and business perceives the health and future outlook of the economy. I looked into how they acquired this data and what was done with the information; which data was gathered, and by whom, and what they do with it once they have it.

I was astounded to discover that *there was no sophisticated formula*. It was much more art than science or mathematics. Sometimes the formulation was more sophisticated than what I grasped, but at least I focused scrutiny and daylight on the major elements—a process which up to that time was as mysterious and opaque as Merlin's book of favorite incantations.

Things were no longer anonymous, and I was considered quite effective with my assignment. In the process, the Department, and no doubt I, stepped on quite a few official toes. SESA was not greatly loved in a number of circles, particularly by the career bureaucrats. However, people were now visible and therefore accountable.

Eventually, Joe Wright moved over to the OMB (Office of Management and Budget), where he became Deputy Director and later Director of OMB. He was replaced at SESA by Edward Failor, who was a central figure in the Nixon Administration. I worked well with him, and we really enjoyed working together. He promoted me, and gave me awards, along with pay increases.

This job continued for a couple of years. Then, Watergate happened. After the Watergate scandal broke, and President Nixon eventually resigned on August 9, 1974, a lot of political appointees were leaving their jobs or shuffling around, creating vacancies. Some people left government altogether, and that resulted in openings. There was a general time of turmoil with many people disillusioned and literally leaping at the opportunity to quit government for the private sector.

In the highly-charged political environment following Nixon's resignation, the Social and Economic Statistics Administration had a gigantic target on its back. In that adversarial political atmosphere, there was a perfect opportunity to do away with it entirely. In reality, the Department was just ruffling too many feathers. Watergate provided the opportunity, if not the justification, and it was ultimately dissolved in 1975. No doubt, a lot of government people were happy to see it go. The employees working in it, including me, were all reassigned.

26—Crossing the Line–Baptism

After the White House Conference, I began my new job with SESA (The Social and Economic Statistics Administration). On my own time, and as I continued to read the New Testament regularly, I was pursuing my investigation of the world's highest profile religions and their sacred books.

During that spring of 1972, I had an epiphany that substantially clarified things for me. I was reading the New Testament, and the fact suddenly dawned on me. *'Wait a minute! The New Testament was written by different people, yet it all fits together seamlessly as one book! Even though there are various authors writing at different times and decades apart, it still feels like one book, one author, and it is all one philosophy!'*

I knew this before, but its significance didn't initially occur to me. At the time, I dubbed it, "the ring of truth!" It motivated me to go back and take another look at the Old Testament. I already knew the stories, and I had a great respect for the prophets. *'When I read the Old Testament, does it have the same ring of truth? Does it sound like the same author?'*

That question led me to seriously read the Old Testament from an entirely new perspective. I needed to know if the same continuity was there—looking at it from that viewpoint. After additional reading, I concluded this was *also* true of the Old Testament. It was written by different people, over a much longer period of time—centuries—and yet it is one comprehensive book that entirely has the feeling of one author. It was a very subtle thing, but it was definitive, and the issue was settled for me.

Having reexamined the entire Bible from that perspective confirmed my faith. *'Yes, it's true.'* I got the same mellow feeling no matter which portion of the Bible I was reading—Old Testament or New Testament. The amazing thing was that it very much seemed to me like the *same* author—the Old and the New

Testament—one Book, one Author. For a Jewish man, this was quite a conclusion.

Whether I read the Old Testament or the New Testament, I was getting a mellow feeling that I didn't receive from the other religious books I read, such as the Koran, the book of Mormon, or even the Apocrypha.

If I read the Bible long enough, a peace would come over me. It didn't make any difference where I was reading in the Bible, I had a feeling of reassurance. During much of the investigation period, with so much uncertainty at work, reading the Bible would calm me down without fail. None of the other books did that.

It also left me with a conclusion—the Bible *is* the Word of God, and the others just don't make the grade. They didn't have that ring of truth to them; they didn't have prophecy. That was essential for me. Without predictive prophecy, there is no evidence a particular religion isn't just some man-made contrivance.

Even though I was continuing the "investigation," by the time I came to the latter religions, I was pretty skeptical from the time I first walked in the door. As June rolled around, I was increasingly convinced that placing my faith in Jesus as my Messiah was the correct decision. I ceased to wonder if I had fallen for some Gentile propaganda.

However, there was one exception—one hurdle I could not cross. *I was not going to get baptized!* There was a reason why the baptism took so long. I struggled with it for 15 months. This issue had really been a stumbling block.

I knew that if a Jew is baptized, the Jewish people are through with him. Up until this time, I was considered a Jew who had non-conformist ideas, and who was trying to sort it all out. But, I had never belonged to a church and I'd never been baptized. I was aware there was a certain tolerance within the Jewish community. However, I was skirting the edge, and I knew that once any Jew pulled that particular plug of baptism, *that most certainly tears it.*

There is no going back. The Jewish community and my own family will never regard me the same way.

I instinctively knew, *'Paul, if you go and do this Gentile, goyishe thing* (Yiddish term for someone/thing which is not Jewish) *of getting baptized, that tears it. It's one thing for you to be curious. It's another thing for you to be investigating. It's yet another thing for you to come to a conclusion. But Paul, when you do this, you have jumped ship completely.'*

Up until this time, I was considered a Jew who had non-conformist ideas, and who was trying to sort it all out.

I knew that in the eyes of the Jewish community, my family in particular, baptism would tear it. Baptism is the final blow. I knew what would come next. *"You've crossed the line. You've completely bought into this, and we're through with you."*

This would be an irreversible thing.

So, there was an internal struggle within me over what other people would think about it. I was giving great consideration to the stakes of the public commitment. But, there was something else going on—an internal struggle. *'Are you absolutely sure you are correct, Paul?'*

That was the reason why I was doing all the reading and investigation of other religions and their sacred books. I wanted to be sure. It was so very important to be *certain* that this New Testament message was not man-made opinion. I needed certitude that these other religions weren't equally valid and I had not allowed myself to be unfairly convinced. I needed to possess certainty within myself. And, over a year or so, at some point, for me it became irrefutable.

In the back of my mind, I was thinking, *'The more you commit to this Paul, the more you are facing a rejection by the Jewish community that will include all your friends: your friends in Chicago, your political friends, probably everybody that you have met so far in the Washington, DC area, and your family.'* All of my friends were Jewish, and of course, my family. Everyone except the political people. These two things were at play, this irrefutability that I had actually embraced the truth, plus my knowledge of the implications of letting everybody—Jewish friends and family—know where I stood.

I really wrestled with this decision, but there was no escaping. *'Paul, if you're going to do it, you have to go all the way. If you're going be a believer in this, then you have to actually believe this is what the Lord wants you to do. It can't be a theoretical thing. You have to genuinely do what you think the Lord wants you to do. You can't hesitate.'*

Also, there hadn't been an opportunity to go and do it. I wasn't ready for it, and there wasn't an opportunity because I certainly didn't want Susan to know that I was doing such a radical thing. Once I finally made the decision, I was just going to quietly go and do it because God wanted me to. I did not want it to be a big deal. It wasn't a deep dark secret, but I certainly wasn't advertising it either.

I was only marginally crossing over. It wasn't something I was delighted to do. I was cornered. Nobody pushed me, but I saw it in the Bible. I wanted to please the Lord, and it was something that I knew I *had* to do. There were a lot of fortuitous things happening to me for which I was very appreciative. *'This is so real, dare I trifle with it? I better go the whole way, regardless of what anybody thinks! No matter what I say, they're gonna think I'm damn nuts anyhow. Paul, you better pull up your socks and just do it.'*

Then an opportunity presented itself. Susan was almost never away, but one weekend in June, with school out, she took our two boys and headed to Chicago to visit her mom and our family. While she traveled to Chicago, I was alone for the weekend. That's when I decided, *'This is the opportunity for you to finally get this done.'*

That Sunday, I walked out my front door, and locked it. I was ready to go get baptized. As I made my way to the car, I had a thought which led me to freeze in my tracks. *'I bet that guy on the bus would really like to hear from me. I haven't spoken to him in over 15 months.'*

I had resolved never to take the bus again. I bought a car to avoid the bus. I remembered his name—*Ray McCauley*—so, I looked him up in the phone book and I called him.

"This is Paul Liberman. Do you remember me?"

"Oh, yes, I do remember you." So, I proceeded to fill him in on what I'd been doing for the last 15 months.

"You know, Paul, I've been praying for you for a long time. That's why I remember your name. I thought our conversations were very unusual and interesting. I noticed you have never taken the bus again. I've often wondered about it."

"Ray, I must tell you, your booklet was mighty persuasive. It was the entire subject of prophecy that caused me to read one of the Gospels, and that led me to pray to receive my Messiah. That set me on a course to where I was able to see God acting on my behalf. Also, I've been studying other world religions, which have further confirmed to me that what you were saying was indeed correct."

"So where to now, Paul?"

"Actually, today I'm on my way out of the house to go get baptized. As I was about to leave, I thought of you. I thought you'd

be interested in learning how our conversations on the bus had completely changed my outlook, my understanding, and my life."

"Where are you going to get this baptism?"

"I don't know. The first church I come to, I suppose."

"Would you mind if I come along?"

"Sure! That sounds great!"

"You know, Paul, they don't all have a baptismal."

"I didn't know that." How could I know? Only once in my life had I even been inside a church. I had just assumed.

"Actually, most churches don't have a baptismal. But, I know one that does, and it's a non-denominational church. I think it might still be open. If not, I think we can get it opened for you to have your baptism.

"Paul, you don't have to do it at a church. I know that's an important issue for you. If you want, I can help you out to where you don't have to go to a church if you would feel more comfortable. We can even do it at your home, in your bathtub."

Within my own thoughts, I quickly weighed the merits of his offer. 'Paul, if you're going to do this thing, let's do it right. You're only going to do it once, and that's it. Let's do it right. Let's make sure you have really done this.' Once I had worked my way to the point where I made the decision, 'I'm going to do this,' resolution took over. 'I'm gonna do it right, no questions!'

"Ray, let's forget about the bathtub."

"In that case, I can take you to a place. If you want, I can drive you there." It made sense as he knew the location of where we were going.

> 'Paul, if you're going to do this thing, let's do it right.'

As we're driving, we were talking. Since it was the weekend, and so little traffic, it only took about 40 minutes. *"Paul, are there any questions about this?"*

I had already thought this through from every direction possible. I had made my decision. *"No, I think I know what I'm doing."*

"Paul, there is one thing that I might want to tell you. Do you remember reading in the Bible about these guys that were praying in tongues. Has anybody ever explained that to you?"

"No, not really."

"Well, this is how it works. At your baptism, when you come up out of the water, it may happen that some strange phrases might come into your mind. They won't even make sense to you, but whatever syllables come into your mind, just say them. Maybe you'll only have one or two or three. Whatever it is, just say those syllables out loud, and more syllables will come to you. Just do your best to vocalize those syllables. No matter how fast or how slow they come, just say them. After a while, you'll become less self-conscious and it'll be a flow of syllables. Just say them. They're meaningful to God. You cannot speak one thing and do reasoning or arithmetic at the same time. And, while you're doing that, thoughts will come to you, and those are usually godly thoughts. This is a way of expressing that which you don't know how to put into words. When you come up out of the water, just remember that.

"But, for this to happen, you have to be willing. So, if you feel like that's something that is good with you, just let it go. It's like in the book of Acts, where people spoke in another language. Now, you won't understand that language. At first it will be very halting, but as you lose yourself in it and focus on God, it will flourish and become natural as though it were a spoken language. If that happens, let it go and embrace it. Just voice the syllables."

While Ray drove, I pondered what he was saying. Whatever this guy was saying, I was trusting it was the truth.

So, we arrived at this non-denominational church, Christ Church, located in the Washington, DC area. Since it was Sunday afternoon, it could have been either open or closed. When we drove up, there was just one car in the parking lot. In fact, there was only one man, and he was in the process of locking up. We arrived just before he would have closed up and left.

Ray called out to him, *"Just a minute, we have someone here who wants to get baptized."*

The guy looked at us and shrugged a bit. *"Sure, come on in."*

Then an odd thing happened. Ray is the one who was going to baptize me. As we were preparing and getting dressed in the garments they had available for this purpose, out of nowhere, and without explanation, a handful of people began to straggle in. They just meander in for no particular reason, and sit down to observe. Now, the service was over—this was in the afternoon. When we first showed up, the place had already been vacated except for the caretaker.

I'm making note of this and wondering about it. Then a few more people came in. I just couldn't understand why. There was no reason. But, I didn't care, I just didn't care. They're continuing to wander in; one, two, five, and so on. By the time I came out of the back in my garment, there were at least 10 people.

As I came up from the water, I didn't know what to expect. What Ray told me on the drive to the church had completely left my thoughts. But, he was *right!* As my head came up out of the water, these unintelligible words started coming into my mind. I recalled what Ray had said, and I yielded myself to what was happening. By that time, my assumption was that he knew what he was talking about. And, it *did* happen exactly as he said it might.

It was very halting at first. The syllables came out and I just kept on going. As fast as they came, the more I kept on going, and the more this language was pouring out. I was speaking faster than I could think of the syllables. At some point, I just let it go, just as Ray had suggested. I went on and on, for several minutes, speaking in tongues. I was amazed, because it was just rattling out of my head. I was going off and I didn't want to stop, because I absolutely felt like something extraordinary was occurring.

I didn't discover until quite a bit later that this was at all unusual. I had no idea there was a dispute about it. In the 1970s, the whole issue was quite a big thing—the Charismatics and non-Charismatics. But for me, it was settled early on. It was never an issue.

I closed my eyes for the baptism. Meanwhile, more people continued to stroll in and to sit down. By the time I came up out of the water, and the whole process was finished, I opened my eyes and looked up, and there were perhaps 20 people who had wandered into the church, sitting in the audience, observing what was going on. It was a non-denominational church, and all these people just meandered in for some reason. As a result, instead of Ray and the caretaker and me, my baptism was actually observed by quite a crowd of witnesses.

I didn't discover until quite a bit later that this was at all unusual. I had no idea there was a dispute about it.

27—First Contact–Other Jewish Believers

After my baptism, Ray McCauley and I promptly struck up a friendship. Right away, I discovered he was a Bible teacher. *"Paul, I go to a church in this neighborhood. Have you started going to a church?"*

I was cautious with my response. *"Well, no."* A flurry of thoughts rushed into my head. *'Is this it? Now that I'm baptized, do I start going to a church and slowly become a Christian—a Gentile?'*

Fortunately, Ray didn't press me, but was very patient. *"Actually, I go to this church because I'm a teacher. I teach a Bible study before the services. Anytime you would like to come, you might find it interesting."* But, there was no pressure—no pressure at all from this guy. I couldn't help but contrast his manner with my former Mormon supervisor. Ray McCauley was giving me space—room to breathe and to find my own way. This freedom to choose—to decide—was very attractive to me. This became the nature of our relationship. With me, Ray would always permit it to be a choice. I really appreciated that.

"Paul, every Sunday morning we get together before the services. If you want to, you'd certainly be welcome. You might find it interesting. For example, you can come this Sunday, or another time, as you would prefer. Just let me know."

There was something about the way he offered. I didn't want to refuse anything from this man. He wasn't pressuring me. He wasn't even asking me really, but he was presenting a possibility. That was his approach to things. He had correctly sized me up.

I hesitated only for a moment. *"Actually, I guess I wouldn't mind."* I knew he wanted me to come to his Bible study, and I wanted to be courteous to him. *"I'll do it."*

The next weekend, I arrived at the church where he taught the Bible study. I didn't know what to expect, but the room was full where it was to be held. There were at least 25 people there: men and women, waiting for Ray to begin. I noted they all seemed very attentive to what he had to say. I also found the subject and his teaching very interesting.

Afterwards, Ray made it a point to escort me around. He seemed aware of the uniqueness of this environment for me. *"So, Paul, I'm glad that you enjoyed the Bible study."* As he escorted me, he offered an additional invitation. *"This is where we have our main services. I attend here every week. If you ever are in the mood, and you want to see what this is all about, we can do that."*

I was there to hear Ray teach. I hadn't expected anything more. However, Ray handled me with such gentleness, plus I didn't want to disappoint him. I wanted to please him. He continued, *"But, if you wanted to go in this week that would be okay, too. It's your call."*

That's how he did it. He was very gentle in leading me. So, I went in for what was to be the regular church service. They started with the hymnal. All the songs were from the 1700s and 1800s. The church hymns really turned me off. I suppose I was visibly squirming in my seat. It all just seemed so *Gentile*. I was not yet at home with Gentile things. It was all so challenging. It seemed like such a formal, churchy thing to do. I didn't want that. In my own mind, it was so *in my face* that I had done something contrary to my people and to my heritage.

Following the music, I listened to the sermon. The speaker's message really reached me. It was quite good. Afterward, as Ray and I were in the car on the way home, he said, *"Paul, if you enjoyed the Bible study, you should be aware that I teach another one during the*

> I was visibly squirming in my seat. It all just seemed so *Gentile*.

week. I teach out of my house if you ever want to come." I didn't immediately respond, but 15-minutes later, as I was getting out of the car, Ray followed up. *"We meet on Wednesday nights at seven o'clock. Do you think you might want to come sometime?"* This was his approach.

This time I answered. *"Well, sure. Why not?"*

"It might be easier for you than going to the church." I guess my discomfort at the church was more obvious than I realized. As it turned out, Ray was very considerate to the fact I was a Jewish guy. He also understood I have a real strong, independent streak. I suppose that was obvious. It was apparent to him I was uncomfortable in his church, but he didn't reproach me about it.

That same week, I attended his Wednesday night Bible study. Again, it was well attended. He was a very engaging teacher. As he was a lawyer—not a religious guy—I found his teaching very thought-provoking.

After this, I sometimes went to church, and I began to enjoy it. By the time I was baptized, I had pretty much run the gamut in my investigation of other religions. That all ceased. Instead, I spent my extra time reading and studying the Bible.

One July afternoon while we were together, Ray casually dropped into the conversation something that totally grabbed my attention. *"Paul, have you ever met another Jewish believer?"*

"No, I haven't."

"Well, I was just talking to a friend of mine and he mentioned he knows another Jewish believer."

> **"Paul, have you ever met another Jewish believer?"**

I was all ears. This was *great* news. *'There's another person on the face of the earth that sees this like I do. I am not alone!'* It had been a lonesome journey for a long time.

"I want to talk to your friend, right away!"

Ray gave me the number of the friend and he was expecting my call. *"Yes, Paul. Ray told me about you. My Jewish friend is Sandra Sheskin. Her parents are both Jewish, and she is a believer. She lives in the Washington, DC area."*

I was amazed there would be another Jewish person who accepted the New Testament and Jesus as the Messiah. *"Well, how do I get in touch with her?"*

"My Jewish friend is Sandra Sheskin. Her parents are both Jewish, and she is a believer."

I lost no time calling the number for Sandra Sheskin. When I reached her, I mentioned the gentleman's name who gave me her number.

"He told me you are also a Jewish believer in the New Testament and Jesus. I'm a Jewish person who has received the Messiah. I'm a believer. I must tell you, I was delighted to find there was someone else who is Jewish and believes the way I do."

"Paul! It's not just me. There are others, too!"

I told her a bit about my spiritual journey, including how I recently reconnected with Ray McCauley. At that time, in 1972, Sandra was around 30. She had been a believer since she was 13. Her Jewish mother was also a believer. Sandra's father, a Jewish man, had divorced Sandra's mother because of the issue of his wife becoming a believer. But, Sandra and her mother were committed to their faith and they refused to compromise.

"Sandra, you said there are others, too?"

"Oh, yes, Paul! I have their names and addresses. We have an association called the Hebrew Christian Alliance of America. I

have the names of the Jewish believers in Washington, DC and Baltimore, and we meet a few times a year."

"How many other Jewish believers are there?"

"Well, there are at least a dozen in our area."

After that, Sandra told me there was a weekly Bible study at her house. A few of these other Jewish believers showed up; however, not all of them attended the weekly meeting.

I lost no time making an appearance at one of Sandra's home Bible studies. The first time I visited, it was Sandra, her mother, and two or three other people, as well as myself. In the weeks that followed, it became apparent that Sandra was clearly the knowledgeable one. However, she seemed to be thoughtful about not wanting to put herself forward as the leader.

It was more of an unstructured discussion group than a Bible study, although we did get into the Bible. Different people would bring up various biblical topics for discussion, and we would dialog about them. It was somewhat leaderless. On occasion, I would take off on some subject, make my case, and ask questions. But, I was not the leader of the group, and Sandra was not the leader of the group. Even though she was the most solid believer among all of us, there was always sensitivity on her part to foster a place for people to come and to feel at ease. She was deliberate not to let it become *"her thing."*

From the time I first connected with Sandra Sheskin, my spiritual focus began to shift away from the Bible studies at Ray's home to the Bible studies and discussion group at Sandra's house. Ray McCauley was very aware of the difficulty I was having with the Gentile nature of the church. Fortunately, Ray was gracious enough to help me find a way to develop my relationship with the Messiah without feeling the need to possess me like some sort of spiritual trophy. He always permitted me the space to find my own way. I will forever be grateful to Ray for that kindness.

28—Early Evangelism–Conflict with Jewish Community

Everyone who knew me could see the evolution underway in my life. At the Commerce Department, I'm telling anyone who will listen what has happened. I tell them about moving to Washington, DC, and about the bus ride, and Ray McCauley. I tell them about my spiritual quest investigating the world's major religions, as well as my conclusion that the Bible stands alone as the Word of God. I tell them I'm Jewish, but that I believe in the New Testament and that Jesus is the Messiah. Whoever will listen, I'm discussing the significance of prophecy as the great authenticator—the unique aspect of the Bible that distinguishes it from all the sacred books of the world's other religions.

At home, Susan sees me reading the Bible—no longer to investigate, but to study. She also sees I'm reading biographies and testimonies of people who have had a spiritual revolution in their own lives. I'm particularly interested in the stories of other Jewish believers. For example, Arthur Katz's story, *Ben Israel—Spiritual Odyssey of a Modern Man*[1], really affected me.

The meetings at Sandra Sheskin's home introduced me to an entirely new network of Jews who believed as I did. This was particularly exciting, as the single most difficult personal barrier I continued to encounter was reconciling my new faith in the Messiah with my heritage as a Jew. I was constantly reminded of this apparent incongruity whenever I would attempt to discuss "the subject" with my parents, grandparents, and even in my relationship with my wife, Susan.

Sandra Sheskin was my link to this potential expanding world of other Jewish believers. At one of the home meetings, I asked her, *"How can I meet some of these people? I'm really hungry to meet other Jewish people who are believers."*

"Paul, a few times a year, we get together with the group from Baltimore. Rev. Casuto will be bringing 15 to 17 people from that group. Next time we get together, you should come."

Not long after, we did meet for one of the combined gatherings. Reverend Casuto played the guitar and also preached. So, I did meet some of these people, however Baltimore was

"How can I meet some of these people? I'm really hungry to meet other Jewish people who are believers."

too distant to be practical for building long-term relationships. But, I continued to take advantage of every opportunity to meet other Jewish believers.

I soon learned more about the history of the Jewish believers in the United States. Beginning in the 19th century, a number of Christian denominations made a special effort to reach out to the Jewish communities with the Gospel message and literature. When these efforts were successful, and Jews came to believe the New Testament message and in Jesus as the Messiah, the new Jewish believers would typically become "members" of the same churches and denominations that had reached out to them. I also learned that as a result of the combination of two factors, these same Jewish believers frequently assimilated into the churches and soon lost all of their identity as Jews.

The two factors were, first, the rejection by their families and friends of their "new" faith, and second, the lack of "appreciation" by Christians and denominations for these new believers' Jewish culture and heritage. In many cases, there was subtle pressure to assimilate and distance themselves from the Jewish community, which of course, included their own families.

By the early 20th century, some of these Jewish believers arrived at the conclusion they had one thing in common. Although from many different denominations (churches), they shared a Jewish heritage and a Jewish culture they did not wish to lose. In 1915, this realization led to the formation of the *Hebrew Christian Alliance of America*. Local Alliance chapters were formed in various communities across the country, which would then become a point of connection with other Jewish believers.

When I first met Sandra, she mentioned the *Hebrew Christian Alliance*. Sometime in September of 1972, she pulled me aside after one of our weekly home meetings. *"Paul, we need to have officers for the Washington, DC Alliance. We need to get more organized—become more active as a branch. I wonder if you could come over next week sometime. We can discuss this, and I would also like for you to meet Sid Roth."*

Sandra had previously told me about Sid Roth, but I had never met him. Sid and his wife, Joyce, were both Jewish believers. Sid was heavily involved in the Full Gospel Businessmen's Fellowship—an organization founded by Demos Shakarian in 1952. Sid had become a believer about the same time as me. It was so "unique" for someone from our Jewish background, that his spiritual journey inspired many. Sid made the rounds of the Full Gospel Businessmen's circuit giving his testimony. Telling his story of a Jewish man who had accepted Jesus as Messiah, Sid had practically achieved celebrity status.

Sandra had been a Jewish believer for over 15 years. Suddenly there appeared on the scene two Jewish guys who are new believers and are also credible people. We had respectable jobs. We didn't come off like nuts. She wanted us to get together to help make this Alliance chapter really active—to make it into something more than a paper organization.

Later in the week, the three of us convened at Sandra's home. After the introductions, Sandra began to explain, *"Technically, we have a branch of the Alliance. It's called the Hebrew Christen Alliance of Greater Baltimore and Washington, DC. However, I believe it would be good for the branch to be more active and not just a paper organization. To get started, we have to have real officers. I've decided that Sid, you should be the president and Paul, you should be the vice president."*

I'm listening to Sandra explain this, and I'm thinking, *'Well, Okay. Sid has experience with more of the Christian community than I do. He's certainly well known in the Full Gospel Businessmen circles. But he hasn't been a believer any longer than I have.'*

At the same moment as I'm contemplating this, Sid responded to Sandra, *"I don't know about Paul being vice president."*

I was taken aback. *"Well, why?"* I asked him.

Without any hesitation, he responded, *"I don't know how strong you are spiritually."* That caught me completely off guard. There are only three of us having this discussion. I felt like he was talking down to me, and I was somewhat put off by it. But, I didn't say anything.

Later, as I was considering the conversation, I decided Sid's response was competitive in origin. We were both strong personalities. Neither one of us was keen to quickly subordinate our self to someone we had just met. It was just human nature.

That was my first interaction with Sid, but we quickly became great friends and ended up working very well together. We both had skills and abilities that complemented one another. I was useful to him in business, and we needed each other to get something going for the Jewish people. We had that in common.

Within a short time, we met again in order to plan a way forward. This time, we were joined by Sid's brother-in-law, Marc Sircus. Sid's sister and her Jewish husband, Marc, a CPA, had all recently become believers. We were sitting around a table brainstorming ideas about how we might proceed. Our objective was to reach out to—to impact—the Jewish community with the claims of the Messiah.

At some point, I couldn't restrain myself. I was still very much a political guy. I had come off the campaign trail, and I was still thinking of myself as a campaigner. I was very promotional minded and familiar with putting on events, conferences, and organizing functions. I was familiar with generating publicity— creating energy. I knew the ropes of throwing things together, of organizing without a lot of resources. Finally, I suggested, *"Why must we have these little meetings? Why don't we create a large meeting and publicize it? No one knows how few of us there actually are. Not unless we tell them."*

There was no disagreement. Sandra considered what I said and then responded. *"Paul, how do you think we should proceed?"*

> **"Why must we have these little meetings? Why don't we create a large meeting and publicize it?"**

"Let's print up 2,000 flyers! They will say, 'Who is the Passover Lamb?' We can put them everywhere; anywhere they will be seen by the Jewish community!" We were all in. Enthusiasm began to build at the very suggestion. Everyone was up for an aggressive approach to sharing the Jewishness of our faith.

Sandra knew how to contact Art Katz, the Jewish believer whose biography I had read. He was living in New Jersey at the time, so we decided he would be the "main event." We put the time and location of the event on the flyers along with the catchy phrase, *"Who is the Passover Lamb?"* We plastered them everywhere! We went right into the local synagogues and tacked the flyers on the bulletin boards—wherever Jewish people would see them.

At this first event, several hundred showed up. It was a tremendous success. As a result, a number of new Jewish believers came out of that event. We were making progress!

For a follow-up, we decided to arrange a showing of the 1968 film, *Dry Bones*[2] that was produced by Shira Lindsay (now Shira Sorko-Ram.) The film pointed out the ancient prophecies and miracle of the rebirth of the modern nation of Israel.

As we were making our plans for that showing, I had a rather unusual experience. I couldn't explain it, but I suddenly had a certainty in my gut that the JDL—Jewish Defense League—would try to disrupt our film showing. I told Sid, *"I believe the JDL is going to crash our event. They're going to march in and cut the electric cord of the projector!"*

Sid looked at me and thought about it. *"Do you really think so?"*

The night of the film, we had just turned on the projector when in marched a formation of more than a dozen members of the JDL! They intended to make a big thing, so they paraded in columns with loud, stomping feet like a platoon, or an army in review. They strutted just like tin soldiers in a Christmas play, all in lock step! Then one of them broke ranks, ran over to the projector, and cut the cord! Then they marched out. They hadn't thought of much of a plan beyond that. However, I was ready! I was so sure they would be coming that I brought along a spare cord. Right away I hooked it up, and we went on with the film without missing a beat!

Sid was in disbelief over what we had witnessed! *"Paul, how did you know that was going to happen? How's it possible? That was supernatural!"* Sid has never let me forget that prediction.

We put on two events, and the numbers were better for each one. I was normally promotional minded, but now we had the bit in our teeth. *"Hey, nobody knows how few of us there are!"*

We concluded that the next event would have a different angle—*"How to Share Messiah with Jewish People."* We brought in Manny Brotman from Florida. After discussing it, we decided Sid should call on his contacts with the Full Gospel Businessmen. His relationships were enormously valuable. I asked Sid to obtain the mailing lists of all the local and nearby Full Gospel Businessmen's chapters. We also lined up all kinds of church lists and anything else we could get our hands on. We were very resourceful. From all of this, we sent a huge mailing throughout the Washington, DC area. For this event, we printed up close to 8,000 flyers, and we distributed all of them.

All of our efforts resulted in a major conference that lasted all day Saturday and all day Sunday. Manny reproduced a seminar he had previously organized that included printed materials he would sell. It was very well presented. We had over 700 people show up. This experience led us to think, *'Hey, this is great! Who cares how few of us there are? We can do this over and over again.'*

The conference was such a success, and generated such interest for Jewish evangelism, we invited Manny to return for an additional evangelistic program. Even though it was just the four of us, we were very promotional minded. We pasted flyers everywhere: *"You don't have to be Jewish to believe in Jesus!"* We even hung some outside the Chabad house. We were fearless.

One of the organizers called on me, and I stood up. I knew I had only one shot and that I was going to get shouted down.

This time the event with Manny Brotman drew about a thousand people.

We were having our meetings, and we were accumulating

> We pasted flyers everywhere: *"You don't have to be Jewish to believe in Jesus!"* We even hung some outside the Chabad house.

the names of people who were interested. Also, there were other new Jewish believers who were joining with us and taking an interest. Out of the woodwork, Jewish believers were coming and introducing themselves. So, we were picking up a new believer here and there and enjoying one another's company. The city was waking up to the idea, *"Hey, there are these Jewish people— Jewish believers."* Word of mouth was helping us build crowds.

When we were holding one of these big events, we would have them in gymnasiums. When you begin with six or eight people, and suddenly you have 15 or 17 adherents, the feeling is, *"Wow! Man, we're really growing!"* We were frankly surprised at how much interest there was in our activities and the degree of awareness we were able to generate. At some point, Sandra showed us a flyer from the group called *Jews for Jesus*. We all thought it was cool that someone else was taking a stand besides us.

By the time we completed a number of these large, public, citywide events, we completely had the attention of the Jewish community. No doubt, we seemed to be larger in our number than we truly were. That was the idea—to get the attention of the community and to create a discussion. Also, we actually were having success, as there were now a number of new Jewish believers as a result of the events.

We were creating quite a stir. In every way we could, we were endeavoring to let people know we existed. That was the point at which the traditional Jewish leadership called for a citywide meeting—all the temples, synagogues, and congregations in the Washington, DC area. It was intended as a meeting to discuss what to do about the epidemic of *Hebrew Christians*.

The Jewish community really turned out! They were alarmed! I don't know how they got so many people to attend, but it was a large auditorium and it was packed. It wasn't just a few hundred people.

Naturally, I wanted to see what the clamor was all about. I was curious. So I showed up—alone—with no one else from our group. There were a number of speakers whose purpose was to explain how dangerous the entire concept of the Hebrew Christian was. One of them warned that a generation of Jewish youth could be lost, assimilated into the church. *"The perpetrators are not Jewish, but frauds bent on deceiving the gullible and less educated of the Jewish youth. They are subverting our people! Their methods are deceptive! Most of these deceivers know very little about Judaism! They're disguised as Jews!"*

This went on for a couple of hours. Emotions were heated. I was just listening and taking it all in. Finally, they came to the question and answer period.

I saw my opportunity, so I raised my hand. One of the organizers called on me, and I stood up. I knew I had only one shot and that I was going to get shouted down. *"Yes. My name is Paul Liberman. I grew up in Chicago. I had a Bar Mitzvah and attended Hebrew school through my first year in high school. I have a question. I want to know what you think about this, which I discovered in the Tenach. It is from Isaiah, and it was written over 2,600 years ago."* Without waiting for a response, I began to read from Isaiah 53.

"He is despised and rejected of men; a man of sorrows, and acquainted with grief: and we hid as it were our faces from him; he was despised, and we esteemed him not. Surely he hath borne our griefs, and carried our sorrows: yet we did esteem him

stricken, smitten of God, and afflicted. But he was wounded for our transgressions, he was bruised for our iniquities: the chastisement of our peace was upon him; and with his stripes we are healed. All we like sheep have gone astray; we have turned everyone to his own way; and the Lord hath laid on him the iniquity of us all. He was oppressed, and he was afflicted, yet he opened not his mouth: he is brought as a lamb to the slaughter, and as a sheep before her shearers is dumb, so he openeth not his mouth."

Suddenly, the building was in an uproar, and they shouted me down. It didn't appear to have made any positive impact, but who knows? I attempted to show them that the Jewish believers weren't cowering in fear of their disapproval. Whatever *they* thought, *we* were going to keep pressing our case.

---

[1]Arthur Katz, *Ben Israel—The Spiritual Odyssey of a Modern Man* (Plainfield, New Jersey: Logos International, 1970).

[2]*Dry Bones*. Dir. & Prod. Shira Sorko–Ram. Maoz, Israel, 1968. Film.

29—Susan's Struggle with Paul's Faith

There was an issue between Susan and me—between husband and wife. We were caught in two different worlds.

After my last bus ride, while reading *Messiah in Both Testaments*, the book given to me by Ray McCauley, I was relating some of it to Susan, but she was not at all interested. I wanted to discuss it, but she just didn't want to talk about it. She shut down on the subject. If there was a religious program on television, she would see that I was tuned in to it—watching. She refused to watch or listen. She wouldn't participate.

Susan saw me reading *Messiah in Both Testaments* at home, and she saw that I was in turmoil. After the parking lot prayer, I bought a Bible. My intention was to read it at the office and at home—basically at every opportunity. I was in a struggle both in my job at the Commerce Department and spiritually. She was aware of all of it.

I've never been a big reader, but Susan saw me reading the Bible with the children, and then I would read the Bible for myself. At first, it was an investigation; eventually, though, it was for study.

For her, this was all very foreign *and distasteful*. I'm sure it seemed to her I was on her case all the time. Susan and I had always enjoyed a very strong partnership, so it never jeopardized our marriage. However, more and more, I was heading in a direction she could not comprehend. For my part, no matter how I tried, I seemed unable to get her to understand. Meanwhile, I was into these Hebrew Christian activities, and she was simply not a part of it.

She was telling some of our friends: *"This has taken a weird turn." "Paul's under a lot of stress." "Paul is going a little off."* Susan wasn't buying any of it.

Initially, I'm sure she believed this was a phase, or a stage, I was going through—eventually, it would go away. I don't know that she had really thought it through, or where this was leading, nor had I. She just had no interest in what I was doing, and I couldn't get her interested. Everything about it was very distasteful to her.

At the same time, I was telling her about thoughts and questions I had and people I'd talked to regarding spiritual things. Then, I was reading the book of Mormon at home. My supervisor was giving me Mormon propaganda, and he wanted to talk about it. Of course, I tried to talk to Susan about it because it affected our life together.

Once I completed the book of Mormon, I told Susan, *"This is not the same as the Bible."* She was catching my commentary as I plowed through all of it. None of it was ever a secret to her.

I attempted to engage Susan in the conversation. However, she did not want to have these conversations. For her, the entire topic was very foreign—*too* foreign. Nevertheless, I was giving her commercials all the time. Yet, I was not getting anywhere. I was not reaching her. In no way was I altering her position. Eventually, I thought, *'I do not see any light on this horizon.'* It seemed hopeless.

Within our little Bible study group at Sandra Sheskin's home, we didn't discuss the rejection issue—it was just understood. *Everyone* had experienced rejection from their families. Everyone understood—we all had this common experience in one way or another. *Our families did not understand us.* Sandra and her mother experienced a particularly tragic case of rejection by Sandra's father as a result of their faith. At least my family back in Chicago was still talking to me. Even so, there was an understanding that I was forbidden to speak about, or bring up, *"that subject"* with them.

I was regularly updating Sandra and the other half-dozen people attending these mid-week studies. We were all praying for Susan. One evening in August, after we prayed, Sandra had an idea. *"Paul, there is an event you could invite Susan to. The High Holidays are coming up and we're going to have a Rosh Hashanah service* (the Jewish New Year that occurs in the fall, 10 days before Yom Kippur—the Day of Atonement). *It will be a gathering of all the Jewish believers east of the Mississippi, and it will be held here in the Washington, DC area. People will be coming from Tennessee, Kentucky, Indiana, Maryland, and many other places."*

That really caught my attention—all these Jewish believers together at one event! I was certainly aware that Susan's greatest objection was the same as almost every other Jew—including my own parents and grandparents. It was a cultural objection. It was the entire Gentile versus Jewish division. *"That is for Christians. I'm Jewish. Jews don't believe in the New Testament and Jesus."* This event would be something to bring Susan to—a Rosh Hashanah service. What could be *more Jewish?* So, I invited Susan to come, and, with almost no hesitation, she agreed.

The event was held at the Miller's house, a sizable, rather large, older home which doubled as their residence and as a venue for meetings. The American Board of Missions to the Jews organized the meeting. This was the same ministry house I visited where I first saw the Jews for Jesus bumper sticker.

> *"That is for Christians. I'm Jewish. Jews don't believe in the New Testament and Jesus."*

The Rosh Hashanah service was conducted in a completely Jewish way. The leader of the services, Dan Rigney from Baltimore, worked for the American Board of Missions to the Jews. For this event, he wore a *kittel* (a white robe used by Jews, especially Orthodox, as a ceremonial garment for men.) The

Hebrew prayers were on point. Dan conducted a first-rate Rosh Hashanah service.

I was especially delighted that there were 40 Jewish believers in attendance in the same place, at the same time, for this holiday celebration. I was so proud. *"Susan, there are 40 people, all Jewish believers! I am not crazy! There are 40 of us! You can see them, Right?"* But she was not impressed.

After the service, we all began to schmooze. Everyone was enjoying the camaraderie. There was one guy who seemed to have a distinct Jewishness about him. I was thinking, *'Now, here's a real Jew. This is not some goyishe Jew. He has "son of Jacob" written all over his face.'* He struck me as a guy with genuine Yiddishkeit—everything about him; his look and his mannerisms. It was Stuart Dauermann, who was originally from Brooklyn. This was the first time we ever met.

After I met Stuart and visited with him for a while, I concluded he was clearly a very friendly fellow. I was then delighted to introduce him to Susan. I wanted to have her speak to him because she could see this was such a very Jewish guy. I believed he would be very impressive to her. One of the primary accusations leveled against my faith was that *it wasn't Jewish!* Susan was in agreement with those people who made this charge. Right here were men and women, clearly Jewish in heritage and culture.

Eventually we left the event, and I was thinking, *'Boy, I really showed her.'* As we were driving home, I asked Susan, *"So, what'd you think?"* I assumed it was all so positive.

Without a moment of hesitation, she responded, *"I have never met such a bunch of schleppers in one place, at one time, in all my life."* (Schleppers—the bedraggled, the poor, the unwashed, and unkempt.) Apparently, she wasn't as impressed as I had hoped. None of it cut any ice with her. She just wasn't buying.

The Rosh Hashanah service was a daytime event. For the previous year, I had been coming home in the evening after work and reading the Children's Bible with my two sons, Joel and Evan. Then we graduated to a more sophisticated children's Bible. By September of 1972, the month of the Washington, DC Rosh Hashanah event, we went to the Scriptures themselves.

Joel was six, and Evan was four. That was our time together every night. They could ask me anything they wanted. I always told them the exact truth as best I understood it and they trusted their dad. It was a natural thing, therefore, when I asked them if they wanted to receive Jesus as their Messiah. There was no reluctance. They both agreed. *"Sure, Dad."* The evening of Rosh Hashanah, Joel and Evan prayed to receive the Lord. Thereafter, they were full-on believers.

Now I had Susan surrounded and outnumbered, because Joel and Evan were after Susan to become a believer. Now they're on her case. *"Mom why can't you understand this? Why can't you see He's the Messiah? How can you say you believe in God but you don't believe in the Bible?"*

It finally all came to a head in January, 1973. One evening, she cut loose at me. *"Look what you've done to our sons!"* She was not liking it.

> *"How can I respect your point of view? At least get the facts before you discount my faith."*

"Look, Susan, you have very strong views, but you have no factual basis whatsoever for your objections. How can I respect your point of view, because you know nothing about anything, and you're not even interested in finding out anything? I can't have any respect for that. At least get the facts before you discount my faith. This has been going on a couple of years now! This is not going away. If you'll acquaint yourself with the facts, and read the New Testament, or at least a portion of it, then okay. Then, if you don't want it, okay, that's fair. But, what you're doing now is not fair. Susan, in the New Testament, there are four versions of what

took place with Jesus. Just read one, and then let's talk about it. Don't you think you could do that, since it has become such an issue between us?"

She thought for a moment about what I had said. Finally, I reached her. *"Yes! I can do that."*

I didn't want to pressure her. Once she agreed to "look into" these matters, I knew it was important to give her space to investigate on her own and to think it through. So, I waited perhaps ten days. One evening, while we were lying in bed, I asked her, *"Do you remember our conversation? Did you do what we discussed? Did you read one of the four New Testament accounts about Jesus?"*

"Yes, I did. I read it."

"So, what do you think?"

"Well it's hard to believe. But, when I think of any alternative explanation, it's even more difficult to believe."

"Look, Susan. Let's say there are only two buttons. One button marked 'it's true,' and the other button 'it's not true.' These are your only two choices, and you have to push one button—you'd push the button 'it's true.' Am I correct?"

"Yes, that's right."

"In that case, being that He is the Messiah, don't you want Him to be your Messiah? Why don't you pray? Would you like to do that now?"

Susan equivocated. *"No. I don't think I want to do that."*

I was attempting to be sensitive and not to push her. *"Would you like to do it privately?"*

"Okay, I can do that."

A few nights later, the boys were asleep and Susan and I were again in bed for the night. It was January 28, 1973. *"So, did you do what we discussed? Did you pray privately and ask Jesus to be your Messiah?"*

"Yes, I did, but, well, actually, nothing happened in my case. I didn't have any dreams, and there were no visions. I didn't hear anything—nothing. I guess it didn't work with me."

"Yes, it did. If you prayed sincerely, it always works. There has never been an exception—never."

"No, Paul. I'm the exception."

"Susan, Honey, if you prayed sincerely, then it worked."

She was silent, but her face revealed skepticism.

I persisted. *"I can prove it to you. I want you to pick out some people—some of our friends—that you believe are very intelligent. Then, I want you to explain to them what you've come to understand. See if they understand what you're talking about."* So, she called up a doctor and his wife with whom we were friendly; a Jewish couple that lived on our block. Susan invited them out to lunch— just Susan and the two of them.

During lunch, Susan proceeded to tell them about her reading exercise and the conclusions she reached as a result. At some point, Susan believed she had given a very cogent explanation. However, two blank faces were staring back at her from across the table. They looked at each other and back at Susan. They weren't getting it. Susan could read their minds. *'What the heck? What's this about? What is going on here?'*

As Susan recounted this later, she was obviously bewildered. *"I don't understand why they couldn't get it."*

"Susan, don't you see what I mean? You told them something that you clearly understand, but they don't get it. That is because it takes faith to understand, and not just facts. You have faith, but they don't yet. That faith came to you the moment you prayed and

asked Jesus to become your Messiah. You have it. That's what I was trying to tell you. It worked. You're not an exception."

"In the future, anytime you begin to wonder whether there has been a supernatural surgery on your head, just find one of our friends, or anyone else, and talk to them about this, and see if they get it or not. That little exercise will certainly resolve your doubt."

30—"You Have a Decision to Make"

When I first arrived in Washington, DC, Charlie Barr clued me in on certain political realities. *"Now, Paul, you have a lot more going for you in Washington, DC than what you realize or what other people may realize. The fact is, there are about 100 people around the country who are in our little cluster—our group. These are people I have helped along the way.*

"It works like this. I make a little bridge for them to walk across. When they succeed, since I've been helpful, I have influence over them. I will always get a hearing from all those people. Now, the fact that you are one of us, Paul, means you will automatically enjoy their support, and they will enjoy your support. Even though many of them have never met you, the fact that you are in the group means they can count on your support. And, you will get to know them over time.

"The thing is, there is only one way you can be dropped from the group. If you do something that is not a credit to the group. You have to be as honest as you are today. If the day comes that you are not as honest as you are today, that's when you will be dropped from the group. Everyone in the group knows that. That's why they know that you can be counted on as a person who will never fail, or lack integrity, because you do not want to get dropped from the group, nor do they. Everyone has to adhere to a certain standard. As long as you do, there's a reservoir of support that's available to all of us."

That's what Charlie had going. He was fond of saying, *"At heart, I am still very much a farm boy, so I observe the nature of things—and I grow people. I try to identify people who are going to succeed, and I try to play a helpful role in their success. You, Paul, are one of those people, as are the other 100 people. The same thing has been true for them. At different times, and in*

different ways, they have all assisted me, and I have helped them."
That's the system Charlie had going.

Charlie did have this knack, which is why he actually became
the godfather of the conservative wing of the Republican Party. As
a result of Charlie's tutelage, there were ten or eleven other guys
who also became kingmakers. They became political consultants.
They were strategists, too, but they all looked to Charlie because
he was older and he had been there first.

Charlie was an amazingly respected person. After I moved to
Washington, DC, I was invited by senators to the Senate Dining
Room to have lunch. Alaska Senator Ted Stevens, Arizona Senator
Paul Fannin, Illinois Senator Charles Percy, and others, invited me
to lunch in the Senate Dining Room. If I went to a reception, U.S.
Senators would routinely recognize me as *Charlie's guy.*

When Vice President Spiro Agnew was having a gala event
for Senator Percy, I was invited. At this event, there was the
characteristic receiving line for Senator Percy. Senator Percy
broke the line, which is not usually done. I wasn't in line, but he
came across the room to say hello to me. I was an Illinois guy and
he wanted to be sure I received a proper greeting.

Congressmen Robert Michael and Ed Derwinski of Illinois,
and Congressman Clark McGregor of Minnesota (a senatorial
candidate who later became the Director of Congressional
Relations for the Nixon White House) were especially cordial and
helpful because I raised money for their campaigns, and/or did
campaigning, but *also* because I was a friend of Charlie Barr. In
addition, the office personnel of Tennessee Senator Bill Brock and
Vice President Spiro Agnew were especially welcoming toward
me because of my association with Charlie. Being Charlie's friend
was a heck of a credential—it was *heady* stuff.

Even after I moved my family to Washington, DC, I was still
seeing Charlie regularly when I made trips back to Chicago,
normally about once a month. Also, Charlie would see me when

he came to Washington, DC, which was every few weeks. So, I was seeing him once or twice a month. When he would come through Washington, DC, we would go out to dinner, or he would come to our home for dinner.

I brought up the subject of spiritual things quite a few times during 1972 and 1973. I was a typical new believer, and I had a zeal for evangelism. The way I saw it, Charlie was my very close friend, and he needed to have his own personal relationship with Jesus. I considered this to be of the utmost importance. It wasn't just a single occasion that I brought up the topic.

I told Charlie that I was Jewish, but I believed in the New Testament. He didn't seem to be interested. On one occasion, he told me he thought the whole thing about Jesus Christ was a myth. Another time, he told me that when he turned 37, his wife wanted him to get baptized. At her insistence he did so, but he assured me it wasn't in any sincere way. Charlie was not a believer as much as I could tell.

But, I continued to discuss the subject with him at every opportunity. I didn't have to be careful with Charlie, because we were genuinely good friends. There was nothing held back between us. I didn't give up. I continued to try to introduce the issue and to show the validity of Jesus, but I wasn't getting anywhere.

I remember one night we were out to dinner, and I was again bringing up the subject of the Bible, and my activities, and my beliefs. I suppose he had just about had it with me on this matter. He responded, *"Listen, Paul, you have a life decision to make, and whatever you decide, nothing is going to change between us. We are friends, and that's always going to be the case. But, you have two possible directions to go.*

"Paul, I believe you have a future in politics. I don't know whether you will be a candidate, an office holder, or if you will be like me—behind the scenes. You are a natural leader, Paul. I can

spot leaders. There are many people who are governors and senators and congressmen—they hold leadership positions, but they are not leaders. I'm a leader, and I can spot a true leader."

At this point, I was naturally flattered, and I was thinking, *'Gee, that is really nice to hear from a guy like Charlie Barr.'*

Charlie paused for effect. Then, he continued. *"Or, you can go and become a Christer. But Paul, you can't do both. If you're going to become a Christer, that doesn't fit with politics. So, you have a decision to make."*

I didn't ponder my response at all. This was not something I had to think about.

> *"Paul, you can't do both. If you're going to become a Christer, that doesn't fit with politics."*

"Well, Charlie, if that's the case, then I'm going to play in the Big Game. There's a two-party system out there in the heavenlies, and that's for bigger stakes. I want to play for those bigger stakes. If that means I have to forego politics, okay. So be it."

Charlie was true to his word. We continued to be friends, and nothing changed. I continued to see him—sometimes in Chicago and sometimes in Washington, DC. We spoke all the time. It was like the ideal father and son relationship. He had a relationship with me that he always wanted to have with his two sons, but didn't. I had a relationship with him that I wanted with my father, but didn't have. It was a very meaningful and fulfilling relationship for both of us.

In 1974, Charlie died at the age of 58 of congestive heart failure. He had congestive heart issues for some time; but if you ever saw him, you would say he was an extremely vigorous guy.

Charlie had it right; I *was* destined for leadership, just not in a way he could visualize. I never regretted it, obviously. As I get closer to the end of life, I can only say, *"Man that was a good decision."*

31—How My Faith Affected My Family

My Father and Mother

After I moved my family to Washington, DC, I returned once a month for a weekend in Chicago. I still had my political connections to cultivate, and there was my relationship with Charlie Barr. On each of these trips, I would see my parents. They heard directly from me about everything that was occurring as it happened. They knew remarkable things were transpiring in my life. I told them how I was getting help from senators and congressmen and about the meeting at the White House. They were also hearing regular updates by telephone about what was going on.

Along with everything else, I would have conversations with my mother and my father that focused on my belief in Jesus and the New Testament. My mother didn't have much to say, but my father certainly did. Whenever the subject came up, he would fly off the handle. He had no tolerance for it whatsoever. It would enrage him. If we got anywhere near the topic, he'd go off the wall—absolutely go off into a tirade.

"You're Jewish, and you ought to stay Jewish. How can you accept all this Gentile stuff? It can't possibly be true."

"But Dad, let me explain to you about the prophecies."

"I don't care about the prophecies. You're Jewish. You were born Jewish. Your ancestors were Jewish. Do you realize that my father came from Russia, and our fathers' fathers suffered for hundreds of years at the hands of the Russian Christians? The Libermans have a history! Where is your loyalty to the Jewish people?"

It all boiled down to peoplehood and status for my father. I was threatening his social standing in the (Jewish) community. That's what it was all about. For him, the very thought was repugnant. It would be the same as if one of my sons, Joel or Evan, came home today and said, *"Hey Dad, I've bought into Hare Krishna."*

My mother was not as strident. One time my mother was visiting us at our home in Virginia. I thought, *'Maybe I can talk to her on a private basis, and then she won't be so intimidated by my father.'* Once I began to explain to her about the prophecies, I thought I was making a convincing case. Then, she interrupted me. *"Paul, stop! You have to stop. You're persuasive—you're very persuasive. I'm concerned. If you persuade me . . . well, I am not prepared to live with your father on the basis of being persuaded by you, so you're gonna have to stop. You like this Jesus thing. It's good for you, but it's not good for me. I'll not hear any more of it."* That was the end of our dialogue.

What was so prominent in her thinking was that her husband would be so terribly upset on a daily basis. He was enraged, *really* angry. And he was very much ashamed of me. He didn't want people to know about his son who was buying into this Gentile religion. This would threaten his whole social standing. Instead, it was the family secret.

She was saying that if she were to be convinced, her relationship with her husband—my father—would be at risk. She was not prepared to face that. She had not grasped the

> *"You like this Jesus thing. It's good for you, but it's not good for me. I'll not hear any more of it."*

long term, eternal, ramifications of this decision. She was considering her standing with my father, but to me the stakes were much higher. This was actually Heaven or not.

Once my father was flying off the handle, there was no more talking to him about it. However, I wouldn't give up. The next visit, a month or six weeks down the road, I'd gently try to broach the subject yet again. It would all start innocently enough. They'd ask me, *"How are you doing? What are you doing? How are the children? How are things in the Commerce Department?"*

Inevitably, the subject that was on my mind was going to come out of my mouth. They began to hear a biblical thread running throughout my thinking. If I got anywhere near the forbidden material, there was combustion. I didn't need to quote prophecies with my father. If I got within fifty feet of the topic, my father was off. He would go totally off.

For example, I would say, *'Thus and so happened, and it was something I had been praying about!"* And, wham! That would do it! Anything near the issue, and he was off and running. Any reference that reflected spiritual content in the slightest way would set him off.

My father was 63 when he retired and sold his portion of the business to his brother. Afterward, he lived pleasantly, but with ill health until he was almost 75. He and my mother eventually accepted that my faith was a part of me. They saw that my life had turned out good. They eventually accepted this for me—but only for me personally.

"If it makes you happy." But they didn't want to discuss it. That was the unwritten rule. One night we were talking when I said to my father, *"One of us is being wise and one of us is being very foolish."*

He stared at me for a moment and then responded. *"That's very true."*

My father had inherited the small family electrical business and was able to keep it going. While I was in Washington, DC, I started a business from dead scratch and with nothing. My father didn't feel he could have done that. It got to the point where I made more money than he did and had more money than he had. From a monetary point of view, I had his respect. He had always had confidence in my competence; but after I became financially successful, he talked to me differently. And the relationship changed accordingly. I never reached the level of appreciation from him I would have liked, but I knew I had garnered his respect.

In Washington, DC, I had an accountant who was a friend as well as a believer. One day, we were discussing my father and my relationship with him. This accountant began to relate a story about a friend of his who had a troubled relationship with *his* father. This guy decided that if his father couldn't do anything about it, he would pull up his socks and go hug his father and tell his father *"I love you."* He was scared, but the guy did it; and he challenged the accountant to do the same thing with his own father. So, the accountant did it. He went to his father, hugged him, and told him that he loved him. The accountant said he was plenty scared; but he did it, and he was glad that he did.

The accountant who was telling me all of this paused and looked firmly into my eyes. *"Paul, I'm telling you this story because you have the same situation going on with your father. You can't have a relationship, because he doesn't know how. If there's gonna be anything more, you're gonna have to make it happen."*

I knew he was challenging me to go and do the same. And, I was so scared—frightened at the thought. People in our family did not hug, let alone kiss. It was just not done. In all my life, my father had never told me that he loved me—never.

After the conversation with my accountant friend, I was in my father's apartment in Chicago for a visit. That's when I decided, *'Paul, what's wrong with you? Do these guys have more guts than you?'* I was actually trembling and my knees were shaking. It was so out of course with the way we normally behaved around each other.

We were in the living room, and I was thinking, *'It's just like marrying Susan. Just take the plunge.'* So, I walked over to my father. He saw me getting closer and he became disoriented. I'm coming right toward him. He didn't know what I was going to do. I was in his personal space. He's thinking, *'What is this all about?'* But I just kept walking toward him. When I got very close, I put my arms around him and I said, *"Dad I have to tell you—I love you."*

He just did not know what to do. He didn't know what to say. But, I did it. I met the challenge. He didn't respond. He had no words. After that, whenever I saw my father, I would go over and give him a hug, which was not done in our family. From that time on, when the family got together, Paul and Dad hugged, but everybody else extended their hands for handshakes. With the rest of the family, it got to be awkward. Eventually, they had to do it, too! After a while, I began to get the idea that my father *did* enjoy my company, and he looked forward to seeing me. I actually think he was proud of me. Even though he did not agree with my faith, he felt that I was leading a good life.

In 1994, Susan and I made *Aliyah* (immigrated) to Israel. I was very shortly at war with the Israeli government over our citizenship, and my parents knew about it. It all had to do with our status as open and notorious believers in the Messiah. But, I was hanging in there for what became a protracted dispute.

I figured, *'God brought me here to Israel—I know it. I'm called here. I'm supposed to do this, and His Word declares that the redeemed of the Lord*

'If the Israeli government is going put me on a plane, they're going to have to forcibly do it.'

shall return. We're the only Jews who say we're redeemed. I'm hanging in there with God; and if the Israeli government is going put me on a plane, they're going to have to forcibly do it. But I'm not doing this to myself—I'm not volunteering. God will come through.' My parents knew about this—that we're in Israel slugging it out. That's when my father tells the family, *"If there's any man alive who can overcome such a situation, it would be Paul."*

That was a tremendous compliment from my father. *"If there's any man alive who could overcome all this, it would be Paul."* From then on, within the family circle, it became a family joke. Whatever it was, *"If there's any man alive that can do that, it would be Paul."* That became my reputation in the family. I always took it as such a high compliment from my father. I had gained his respect, which was always so important to me. However, as a young man, it had seemed so elusive.

In 1994, my father became very ill, and everyone had been called together to say goodbye. I also came in from Israel where we were living at the time. It was in early September, and I had been praying for my father when the thought came to me, *'Your father will not pass from among you during the next year.'*

As I entered my father's room, everybody was kissing him goodbye, because everyone believed he was dying. The doctors were all in agreement that he was dying. But I felt I heard something else from the Lord. It's an unusual thing. I wasn't anticipating anything to come to mind. But, I had a peace about it, so I said, *"Dad I'm not here to say goodbye. I know a lot of people are here, and they're all saying goodbye too early. I don't think you're going now."*

He looked at me puzzled. *"Really?"*

"Yes, I was praying about it and I understood that you're going to be around for this next year."

This turned out to be exactly correct. He lasted one more year.

My mother had also come to respect our family's faith. It wasn't for her, but I know that she had come to respect us. After my father passed away and we had spent nine years living in Israel, we moved back to California. I was working as a stock broker. One day, my mother called me up. *"Paul I have a very important question to ask you. How long am I going to live? It's a reasonable question to ask. How long am I going to live?"*

I was frankly shocked at the question. *"Mother, how can I possibly tell you how long you're going to live? What kind of question is that?"*

"No, Paul. If anyone can tell me, it will be you."

"I can't tell you how long you're going to live. No one can tell you how long you're going to live."

She persisted. *"If anybody can, you can, Paul."*

"But Mom, it's not a fair question to ask me. What makes you think I would be able to answer such a question?"

"Because, Paul, you're a seer. Is that how you say that, 'seer?' You're a seer. You see things."

"Mother, I don't know where you get that."

"Well, I know you're connected to God. I don't want to be connected the way you're connected, but I know you're connected with God." In the end, both my parents accepted my faith, but *only for me.*

My Grandfather and Grandmother

In some ways, I was closer to my paternal grandfather than I was to my father. I had a closer emotional tie with him. But, he was in Miami, so he wasn't so easy to access.

Once, during the 1970s, I made a trip down there just to visit, but I had another agenda item going. I was thinking that they were getting older, and I wanted them to understand about coming to faith in Messiah. I felt a responsibility to present this to them.

So, I invited my grandmother out for a walk, figuring that she was the easier one to talk with. I decided to try it out for size with her, which seemed perfectly natural.

"So. Paul, how are you doing? What's new?"

"Grandma, I've had some interesting new things take place. What's new is, I've come to take more of an interest in the Bible—the Holy Scriptures."

"Oh, yeah?"

"Yes, Grandma, because what has intrigued me is this whole concept of the Messiah in Judaism. What is this all about? I discovered the Bible does predict details about who the Messiah is going to be. For example, whoever is the Messiah, there's going to be a way of recognizing him."

I had her interest. She was not shutting me down. *"Yeah, well, how are we supposed to recognize him?"*

I continued, *"Whoever the Messiah's going to be, he's going to be sold for 30 pieces of silver. And, he's going to have his hands and feet pierced. And, he's going to die for the sins of other people—not his own sin. And, whoever he is, and this is amazing, he's going to be rejected by the Jewish people."*

I was very careful with my language. For example, I was saying "Messiah" instead of "Christ." I went on with several of the Messianic prophecies. I got out about five or six of these prophecies and she was kind of curious, so I kept going. *"What's more, whoever the Messiah's going to be, according to the book of Daniel, he very clearly is supposed to arrive before the destruction of the Temple, which occurred in the year 70 CE (Common Era).*

> *"Whoever the Messiah's going to be, he's going to be rejected by the Jewish people."*

"The amazing thing to me, Grandma, is that the Messiah has already come."

Now I really had her attention. *"Yeah? So Paul, who was he?"*

I fed her half a dozen of the most prominent Messianic prophecies that were unmistakable, but she didn't have much of a background in Judaism. So, she asked, *"Yeah, who was he?"*

"Well Grandma, he's the Jewish Messiah, but the Gentiles call him Jesus. His Hebrew name is Yeshua."

"Really?" She says.

"Really, Grandma."

"How come nobody ever told me this?" At this point, I was feeling very good about the conversation. As we were walking back, I thought, *'Paul, Just let this percolate.'*

That ended the visit, and I returned to Chicago. *The Fig Tree Blossoms[1],* my first book, had just come out with its first printing. I sent my grandfather a copy because I knew it couldn't be a casual conversation with him. It would have to be a more serious thing— more proof than what I was able to give to my grandmother. He would certainly be more difficult to persuade. After all, in Minsk, he was studying to be a Rabbi before they left for the United States.

Within 24 hours of receiving a copy of my book, he returned it. I saw the postmark. It was a *real* fast turnaround. Then, he wrote me, and he was very angry. The reason—in his letter he said *I was busy trying to convert his wife to Catholicism.*

To the Jewish mindset, there is no distinction between Protestants and Catholics. It's all Gentiles. After the letter, I started hearing from the rest of the family that I had been disowned by my grandfather. *"He was my favorite grandson,"* past tense. And, he wasn't going to be talking to me from now on. That was that, and I understood. As much as it pained me, I understood.

He was cutting me off as his father had cut him off. In that case, it had been over my grandfather violating the Shabbat by working—something he had to do to keep his job in the jewelry store. In

> **To the Jewish mindset, there is no distinction between Protestants and Catholics. It's all Gentiles.**

my case, I had breached the sacred wall of the Jewish people by reading and believing in the New Testament and Jesus. Worse yet, I had tried to "convert" his wife to a Gentile religion.

I'm sure that after our walk together, my grandmother came home, marveling at the whole thing. *"Hey, what's this about? Paul was telling me all these things from the Bible about the Messiah. He said the Messiah came, and his name is Jesus."* This is why he was upset with me, and so, I just figured, *'Well, all right. I can't do much about that.'*

I felt badly about it, but I'm continuing on. I'm sure I'm right about the Bible and the Messiah.

A few years passed with this relationship. Then, I had an idea. On Father's Day, I called my grandfather long distance. Why not? It's Father's Day! I thought, *'What's he going to do if I call him? Is he really going to refuse to talk to me? Right.'* So, I called him up.

When he came to the phone, I said, *"Hello, Grandpa, this is Paul."* No answer! But, the line is still live. I hear clearly it's not a dead phone.

"Grandpa, I'm calling to wish you a happy Father's Day." Nothing, no sound, nothing. He's thinking about what to do. I kept going. *"Grandpa, are you there? It was Father's Day, and normally I call my father. But, I thought, 'Why don't I call my father's father? He's a father, too.' You are my father as well as my grandfather. You're a father to me. So, I just thought I'd call you up to give you my loving regards for the day."*

I'm going on with this. Three, four, maybe even five tries at it, and there is not a word—silence. I can almost hear him thinking, *'What do I do? Hang up on Paul? What do I do? On Father's Day?'*

But, I'm not going anywhere. I'm determined to wait for something to happen. The first one to blink, loses. It's up to him. After about four attempts with some pregnant pauses, *finally*, a response. *"Hello? Hello? Hello, Paul, is that you? Paul. Is that you? I think maybe we had a bad connection. Is that you, Paul? Did you call me? Is this Paul? Is this my grandson, Paul?"* He was going with the story that he hadn't heard any of what I had been saying. He had been thinking about it, and this was his cover story.

After the Father's Day call, everything was restored to normal. There was never another conversation about the subject, but he knew where I stood. The loving relationship continued, unimpaired until my grandfather passed away in 1980.

Not long after he passed—six or eight months later—my grandmother also passed away, and I had not been down there to visit her. I never had another private conversation with my grandmother on the subject of the Messiah.

---

[1]Paul Liberman, *The Fig Tree Blossoms* (Indianola, Iowa: Foundation Press, 1976).

32—A New Jewish Congregation

On January 28, 1973, Susan prayed to accept the Messiah. For almost two years, I had made every effort and used every approach to reach Susan with the truth of the New Testament and the claims of Jesus as the Messiah. Now, she was in the fold. In February, she went with me to church—*once.* After that, I couldn't get her to go again. *"I have a headache; I'm having my period; I've got to do these errands."*

She was just not objective. She was demurring. One week would melt into the next. After the first time, I could never get her to go again. I could see these were excuses. It wasn't as if she was throwing up with the flu, or anything.

"Look, Susan, this is not working. You have to feed your faith."

"Paul, I just can't do it. Going to church is just not a very Jewish thing to do."

They were not objections like, *"I don't like that. This is unacceptable."* It was the whole idea of it—the entire concept of—*"I'm going to become a church-goer? Come on!"*

> *"Paul, I just can't do it. Going to church is just not a very Jewish thing to do."*

In her mind, or for any other Jew, there is no distinction between Catholics and Protestants. Like any other Jewish person, her apprehensions could be expressed as; *"Oh, my goodness! I'm going to go to church? I'm going to kneel down at the water fountain, and I'm going to have my own beads and genuflect? No Way! I'm just not doing this!"*

It would be the same as if the Jewish wife's husband came home and said, *"I've decided I'm going to be a Mormon."* Now, you're going to go to a Mormon temple? You're going to learn a special handshake? Or suddenly you are married to somebody who decides to become a Hara Krishna, and now you are going to go dance on the streets with a tambourine?! Come on! This is not reasonable! For Susan, the entire concept was a freak out!

We *had* to grow together spiritually. This was, fundamentally, family survival. Left unresolved, this threatened to blow our entire marriage apart. Something needed to be done, and it needed to be done right away.

At least Susan was now a believer. At last there was spiritual unity in the home. One evening Susan and I were in our bedroom for the night. We were going over this same topic of our faith again when we began to consider, *"We don't want our sons to have a schizophrenic sense of identity. What are we going to do for our boys to help develop their faith and sense of spiritual identity? Are we still Jewish or are we Christian? It doesn't seem correct that we're Christian and still Jewish."* If *we* had difficulty putting it into a box—of explaining it—especially to our friends and relatives, where would that leave our children as they are growing up? Would they be Jewish *and* Christian? Jewish *or* Christian? One point we had no trouble agreeing on—both Susan and I came down solidly on the side of not abandoning our Jewish identity, culture, and heritage.

After a bit more discussion, Susan made an offer. *"I would be comfortable with the other Jewish people from the Alliance. If we can get together with them, I'd be comfortable with that. That would be enough for our family."*

Over the next couple of days, I thought about Susan's suggestion. The more I thought about it, the more I could see it as the answer. I wanted to have a congregation. I wanted to have regular Friday night meetings that we as a family would attend and that we could develop. Mostly, I was thinking about my immediate family—my wife and sons. I was also thinking, *'How will I explain myself to my Jewish relatives and non-believing Jewish friends?'*

A few points were crystal clear in my mind. The congregation needed to be immediately recognizable as Jewish! Jewish flavored: Jewish in origin, and Jewish in content. Not Gentile—*not a church.* Being clearly identifiable as Jewish was of paramount importance. This was abundantly clear starting with Susan's struggle and our discussion regarding the future identity of our sons.

On occasion, during my regular trips back to Chicago, I had visited the First Hebrew Christian Church of Chicago. But, I had something different in mind. That group was affiliated with the Presbyterian denomination. For me, that was a problem.

> *'How will I explain myself to my Jewish relatives and non-believing Jewish friends?'*

I wanted something local that would be self-supporting and definitely *not* affiliated or subservient to a Christian church, denomination, or other Christian ministry. For me, it was self-evident that in order for it to be even remotely acceptable to our families and friends, this congregation had to be Jewish in every way, including the way it was financed.

After the initial idea was formed from Susan's and my bedroom discussion, it seemed the next step would be to confide in Sandra Sheskin and Sid Roth and garner their support. These were the two Jewish believers with whom I was most comfortable. I needed to get them onboard.

First, I talked with Sandra. She was the "most experienced" Jewish believer I knew. I told her about my difficulty in getting Susan to attend a church service, and I told her about the mutual concerns we had as parents raising our children as Jewish believers while maintaining a Jewish identity. The solution seemed obvious to me. But, when I laid out the idea of a Jewish congregation meeting together without connection to or support from a Christian church or denomination, Sandra was less than enthusiastic. I don't know what I was expecting, but that wasn't it.

For Sandra, it wasn't reluctance; it was uncertainty. It wasn't that she was resisting. She just wanted to be sure we weren't stepping off track—the road previously traveled—which we were! We *had* to for the sake of the Jewish people and the Jewish believers to come.

She wasn't against it, but she was *unsure*. What I was suggesting was something new. Would people approve? What would church people think of it? I personally didn't have these questions. For me, the only motivation was the survival of my family. Sandra didn't have these drivers. She was unmarried, and she didn't have any children. Doctrine was very important to Sandra, and she *was* the experienced one, but this was all too new. Sandra just wasn't sure. Finally, she asked me, *"What does Sid (Roth) think about this?"*

Sid Roth was very much involved with and had a spiritual identity with the Full Gospel Businessmen's Fellowship. Sid was the recognized Jewish believer in the Washington, DC area. He was on the circuit. He was called upon to be a speaker at all of the Full Gospel Businessmen's events. He was the known Jewish believer, so I really needed his support.

Sid was just trying to keep his marriage together. Joyce, his wife, was a Gentile who converted to Judaism when they married. It wasn't clear to me where she was spiritually. They were separated when he first became a believer. After he became a believer, he returned to the marriage in order to please God. Sid wasn't certain that what I was proposing was even necessary. However, he had a young daughter and there was an aspect of what we were trying to do that appealed to Sid—the idea that his daughter was friends with and knew my two sons. As a father, he foresaw their future identity as an issue to be considered. He agreed to go along with it.

Marc and Shirley Sircus, Sid's sister and brother-in-law, another Jewish couple who were believers, also had two children. The idea that the children—at least these five small children—would have each other was attractive. However, Sid was not so convinced that he would go out on a limb for it. For Sid, if it had gone the other way and the concept of this Jewish congregation failed, it was all right with him—and certainly it was all right with his wife, Joyce—to go to a church.

Sid didn't have any real drive to do it. His focus was the Full Gospel Businessmen and evangelism. He didn't have a certainty that there was a great necessity for a Jewish congregation. What we were proposing was something new. So, there was this back-and-forth; first with Sandra, then with Sid, and then back to Sandra.

At one point, I was in a telephone booth talking to Sandra about some particular aspect of getting this congregation started, and she was resisting me, not sure. Again, she stated she wanted input from other experienced believers. I got very frustrated with her because I could see this was not going to be smooth. I needed these people to cooperate with me, and she appeared to be giving me points of resistance. At the same time, it was a hot day, and I was standing in a glass telephone booth, the sun magnified tenfold, with no air, sweating and trying to carry on a conversation about something very important to my family and me. As the conversation continued, I was becoming increasingly frustrated. Finally, I lost my temper with her. I blew my cool with Sandra while standing in this steamy, hot, telephone booth.

The point is, there was a measure of resistance. It was not smooth sailing. At times, there were *literally* heated exchanges. Although Sandra and Sid were Jewish, and they were hoping something might come out of it, they weren't fired up like I was—

like I *had* to be. I was hoping for—and wanting—enthusiasm from them, but it just wasn't going to happen. Eventually, I concluded the best that I could achieve was for them to agree to go along.

At some juncture, I suggested, *"As our last meeting of the year for the local Alliance, why don't we have a picnic and invite all of the believers—Jews and Gentiles—we know? Let's ask if there are other people who would be interested in meeting with us in a Jewish style. We will invite everyone in the Alliance as well as others who might either be interested or at least give us some moral support."*

We had already held several public events including two with Manny Brotman and one with Art Katz. At these meetings, there were some people who were interested. We had also come to know some other Jewish believers. Of course, we kept their names on a mailing list.

So, we agreed to organize a picnic under the auspices of the Hebrew Christian Alliance of America. Between 50 and 60 people showed up. It was decided beforehand that I would make the presentation because I was the one with the burden to do this. I had a family crisis with my wife and children—*how is this going to work?* Therefore, I was the one pushing the agenda.

The time came at the picnic when I gathered everyone to make my pitch. *"We've been having these Alliance meetings. We've had a number of successful events. A few of us have been*

"We would like to have a congregation, something that would be in a Jewish style, something culturally familiar and not foreign to those of us from a Jewish descent and heritage."

discussing the future of our association. For the Jewish believers among us, especially those with children, we've been considering how things might work in the future. We would like to have a congregation, something that would be in a Jewish style, something culturally familiar and not foreign to those of us from a Jewish descent and heritage. What we have in mind would be a place where new and prospective Jewish believers could come and feel comfortable. They should have another option if they accept Jesus as their Messiah, other than that they will have to go to a church and become a Christian. In other words, that they will not have to give up their Jewish heritage, identity, and culture, and become a Gentile.

"We would like this congregation, or fellowship, to be conducive for any prospective or new Jewish believer. Also, we would like for our own families to have something of a Jewish style and culture in which to raise our children. We would like to ask for your moral support at a minimum, just acknowledging that this is a good idea. Certainly, we would also appreciate your attendance and participation. Does everyone agree that this is a good thing? What do you think?"

At this point, one guy raised his hand. He wasn't Jewish. *"I have recently heard from the Lord. As a result, for at least a month, my living room has been set up with nothing in it but audience chairs and a podium that has a Star of David on the front of it. I was told a month or two ago to do it, but I didn't understand why. It was strictly out of obedience that I did it. Today, I know why. It was for the purpose of holding the meetings that you're asking for. My living room is already set up and ready to go."*

I had goose bumps. That was a confirmation to everyone that this was supposed to be. For me—a man focused on understanding and recognizing destiny—this had the unmistakable ring of familiarity.

Friday evening, May 18, 1973, was the first time Beth Messiah met. We began to meet, and we didn't know what the heck we were doing. For music, we brought Christian records and someone else brought a record player. We played the records, and we sang along with the words. *"Put your hand in the hand of the Man who stilled the waters."*

We had all the modern (at that time) Christian songs. Sandra, who is a singer, would sing a special song before the message. We didn't know what we were doing. All we knew was that we had 15 people sitting there, and we were going forward.

Sid and I worked out an arrangement whereby one week I would be the moderator, and he would be the speaker. The next week, he would be the moderator, and I would be the speaker. Each of us had been a believer for only two years. We hardly knew anything, but we pressed forward.

I didn't know how to give a message, so I would bring a book or a booklet on Israel or some related subject. Before the meeting, I would highlight different things that I would then read from the booklet. I would read a sentence or two, and I would make some commentary. Then, I would read the next sentence or two—more commentary. That was our message. I was very careful about what I was saying.

Sid wasn't much better. At least he had experience giving his testimony at the Full Gospel Businessmen's meetings. He was very experienced in this, but there are just so many times you can give your testimony—*to the same people!* Also, we would talk about what went on with the Lord during the week, our experiences and so on. That's how Beth Messiah was born in this guy's living room. But, Susan and I always said it was conceived in our bedroom.

33—Christians or Jews?

My reasons for pushing so hard for the creation of Beth Messiah were very personal—some might even say *selfish*. At the core of my being, I believed the success of the congregation meant the survival of my marriage, my family, and my spiritual life.

Experience with my family in Chicago, my grandparents in Florida, and, in fact, with my wife, Susan, all convinced me it was absolutely necessary to maintain and affirm my identity as a Jew. The suspicion, if not the expectation, of all of them was that by accepting Jesus as my Messiah, I had "crossed over" to the "other" side.

I was not alone. Most of the Jewish believers had the same experience. We were examined and scrutinized by our non-believing Jewish family and friends who looked for any evidence that we were seeking to assimilate—to drop our identity and renounce our heritage as Jews.

> ""They're no longer Jewish! They're assimilating! They've embraced a Christian God and a Christian religion! It's the antithesis of Judaism!"

Our opponents in the Jewish community fanned the flames of this suspicion at every opportunity. *"They're no longer Jewish! They're assimilating! They've embraced a Christian God and a Christian religion! It's the antithesis of Judaism!"*

I was born in January, 1942, less than eight weeks after Pearl Harbor. During the first three years of my life, millions of Jews were executed and cremated *because* they were Jewish. As I lived a carefree and safe life crawling around on carpet in a Chicago apartment, other Jewish children my age were thrown *alive* into crematory ovens all over Europe. The Nazis felt it was a waste of ammunition to execute them before disposing of their small bodies.

For my generation, maintaining a Jewish identity was a responsibility—a willingly accepted obligation. We were expected by our parents to insure that the flame of the Jewish people burned brightly into succeeding generations. As a Jewish believer, I came to the conclusion that I was part of a people within a people, a remnant and spiritual seed that continues back to my ancestors: Abraham, Isaac, Jacob, David, and to the Jewish Messiah and King born in Bethlehem of Judea.

When Beth Messiah began, I did not have a "grand vision" or a "big plan." For me, it was fundamentally survival. For my generation of new Jewish believers, expressing and explaining ourselves to our suspicious Jewish families, relatives, and friends became a tactical art form.

For example, our own Jewish experience taught us that there were special words that unnecessarily triggered negative emotions in the collective Jewish consciousness. As Jewish believers, many of us became convinced that the truth of salvation in the Messiah and the New Testament could be communicated better without stepping on the land mines of loaded words.

The most basic item on the "hot" list was what we called ourselves; how we identified. For Jews over the centuries, the word *"Christian"* had come to mean, *"Gentile—one not Jewish, synonymous with Catholic—a follower of the Pope in Rome."*

In 1973, there were about 1,000 Jewish believers in the country. Of that group, there was a small pocket of Messianic Jewish believers who wanted a more Jewish identity, distinct from simply melding into the Church and disappearing.

By the early 1970s, a number of us young Jewish believers, in an effort to relate to the greater Jewish community including our families, relatives and friends, refused to identify ourselves at all as "Christian" or even "Hebrew Christian." My personal conviction was that to do so would be the same as taking out an ad in the Jerusalem Post. *"Paul Liberman is no longer Jewish! He is now a Gentile!"*

Instead, without much discussion, or by prior agreement, we younger, new, Jewish believers identified ourselves as *"Messianic Jews."* For us, it quite simply meant, *"Jewish followers of the Jewish Messiah; believers in the New Testament,"* with an emphasis on *Jewish*. It was an upfront declaration that we had not—and had no intention of—abandoning or otherwise renouncing our Jewish heritage, history, and culture.

I would eventually learn that for decades, dating back to 1915 and to the beginning of the Alliance in America, there was a minority voice among the Jewish believers who preferred not to identify themselves as "Hebrew Christians" but rather as "Messianic Jews."

Two men in particular, Dr. Lawrence Duff-Forbes and Ed Brotsky, had a Messianic vision as far back as the 1940s. By 1973, there were a scattered few (such as Martin Chernoff who had a congregation in Cincinnati) who regularly used the term "Messianic." Also, Manny Brotman, who had been a central figure in two of our public events held in Washington, DC, had an organization with the name *Messianic Jewish Movement International*. For years, Sandra Sheskin had identified herself as a Messianic Jew. Sid Roth described himself as a Messianic Jew from the beginning of the time that he was on the Full Gospel Businessmen circuit. Elsewhere, others used the term "Completed Jew." For some of us, that was a little insulting, because *"You're an incomplete Jew?"*

Sid Roth, Sandra Sheskin, and Manny Brotman—for them the issue was a matter of personal identity. Without a doubt, for me that was true, but I had an *additional* driving motivation for the creation of the congregation. *"How can we have a synagogue that in any way uses the term Christian?"* That made it a pivotal question for me. We were already describing ourselves as Messianic Jews. We were tolerating the "Hebrew Christian" insignia of the National Alliance, but we didn't like it.

Almost as soon as Beth Messiah began to hold meetings on May 18, 1973, I realized I would be required to "explain" our purpose to the outside Jewish community. I needed to be able to honestly profess that we were not an appendage, subsidiary, affiliate, or offshoot of any Christian (Gentile) denomination or ministry. We were a Jewish congregation and always would be. We absolutely were *not* a "church." For this reason, if we identified as, *"Beth Messiah, a Messianic Synagogue"* immediately followed by, *"affiliated with the Hebrew Christian Alliance of America,"* it would seem an inherent contradiction in our stated goal. How could you have a "Christian synagogue?" It was an oxymoron! For me that was a major problem.

The Jewish world was already saying, *"See! They're not Jewish! Told you they weren't Jewish. They believe in Jesus! We told you that you can't be Jewish and believe in Jesus. You see? They've become Christians! They're Hebrew Christians!"* If this fledgling thing—Beth Messiah—was to have a future, it *couldn't* be under the banner—Hebrew Christian Alliance!

I was not alone in believing there was a need for a change—especially in the name of the national organization. For years, numbers of us were describing and identifying ourselves as Messianic Jews—*not* Hebrew Christians. Bringing the national organization's name into conformity was the next logical step. At the core of my being, I was convinced the time had come for the "Hebrew Christian Alliance of America" to undergo a name change.

Be It Resolved

The Hebrew Christian Alliance of America held a national conference every two years. The next was to be held in Dunedin,

Florida, in July 1973. This would be my first such national conference since becoming a believer.

Sometime after Beth Messiah started meeting in May, and weeks before the conference, the local Washington, DC Alliance chapter received a special notice that we were expecting from the national Alliance office. We were notified that appearing on the conference agenda, there would be a motion for a proposed name change of the national Alliance organization which required a change of the constitution. *"Be it resolved: The name of the Alliance shall henceforth be known as the Messianic Jewish Alliance of America."* A motion to change the constitution of the organization had to be noticed in advance of the conference at which it was to be considered by the members.

Everyone who registered for the conference knew the name change was an agenda item. At our local Alliance branch, we were all aware of the proposal, and we all wanted it to succeed. For me, this was not some theoretical question. This had to be, no matter what.

We also realized that, if we didn't do it now, we would have to wait at least two years until the next national conference. What I couldn't know was that there were some long–time Alliance members who, to put it mildly, were not convinced the name change was the correct thing to do. Unbeknownst to our Washington, DC Alliance, the "old guard" was buckled down and ready for a challenge to the status quo. Whatever their persuasion, everyone intuitively understood the real issue. *"Going forward, how are we, as Jewish believers in Messiah, going to relate to Christianity?"*

Dunedin, Florida—The Conference

The national Alliance conference was scheduled for July 1973, and was to be held in Dunedin, Florida, which was less than two months after Beth Messiah began in Washington, DC. I was struggling for the survival of my family. My wife, Susan, was a brand new believer as of January 28, 1973. For me and for others, it's do or die. We must have a Messianic Jewish identity. There was no point having a congregation of Jewish people and then calling ourselves Hebrew Christians. We needed to identify as Messianic Jews to be consistent and for credibility.

Since it was summer, school was out, so Susan stayed at home with our young children. About 250 people attended the conference. There were many young people besides me, all with the same commitment to see this goal accomplished. I was certainly not alone. There were Sid Roth, Sandra Sheskin, Larry Rich, Joe Finkelstein, Joel and David Chernoff, Larry Feldman, and Shira Lindsay (the future Shira Sorko-Ram), to name a few. We were all impassioned with this "Messianic vision." And, there were those who were older such as Martin Chernoff and Golda Sheskin, the mother of Sandra Sheskin, as well as Manny Brotman, who was a few years older than me.

We were all aware that Jeremiah said, *"as long as there is a sun and the moon and the stars, there will also be a distinctive people."* This made it a historical imperative! It didn't seem like folding into the churches was something that was consistent with that Scripture, but the tide and momentum of history and precedent were certainly all against us.

A Revolution

The national Alliance was very tightly structured. During the morning meeting on the first day, there was a reading of the budget. As they read the report, it revealed a loss for the previous two years.

"Are there any questions?"

It was my first time there. I raised my hand. Apparently, it was understood, you didn't do that then. You didn't challenge or question the leadership. I didn't know any better. I had been a believer for barely two years. I raised my hand and stood up. *"What we have heard today is very distressing—that the national organization is showing a loss! I'm new in the movement, so please explain to me, where is this leading us? Why don't we do something about it?"*

I continued on with my little rant, and I sat down. My comments certainly caused a stir as a low murmur could be heard throughout the meeting room. I didn't realize there was an underlying feeling that no one should dare be seen as confronting the key people who, for quite a number of years, had held office.

At lunch, Golda Sheskin came over to me. *"Paul, you've created a revolution and you didn't even realize it. It was waiting to happen, and you didn't know any better. You just put the match to the fuse. You cracked this thing wide open!"*

I had no clue what the heck she was talking about.

That afternoon, there were elections for officers of the national Alliance. Martin Chernoff was elected as the new president of the Alliance of America.

The Resolution

The next day's schedule had the agenda item for which we had all been waiting—*the resolution changing the name of the national Alliance.* We made sure that whoever was sympathetic to our point of view was there. The discussion was lengthy with both sides passionate regarding their position. But there were a lot of them and not many of us. However, we did our best to convince the entire assembly of the significance of the name change.

"Not only are the Jewish believers to continue as long as the sun and moon and the stars as a distinctive people, but how can we have our children growing up with a schizophrenic sense of identity? If all our life effort is to win Jewish individuals to the Kingdom of God just to have them folded into the Church—what

legacy is that, and what credibility does it bequeath the future? It's a dead end rather than a multiplication.

"The credibility of Messianic congregations is that we're not just about evangelism. We also need to build a community. We're a people within a people, and we need to develop our own culture that is a Messianic culture consisting of Jewish believers, which is somewhat different than the Church and somewhat different from traditional Judaism. That all has to happen on a backdrop of self-identity.

"It's different than Christianity because, first of all, the language is not the same. Instead of Christ, it's Messiah. We call Him by His Hebrew name, Yeshua, instead of Jesus. We're sensitized as to how these things sound to non-believing, traditional Jews. We see that a lot of the Church is just running roughshod over all that, with language they don't recognize is flammable. Words that Jewish people cannot hear, because Christianity has been the enemy for so very, very long; for many hundreds, if not thousands, of years.

"The Jewish people were not listening, because they couldn't listen. It was a red cape in front of the bull. As Jewish believers, we need to put our best foot forward and make our best case for the Messiah and the New Testament without negatively prejudicing our case before we ever get started.

"Also, we are different culturally from the traditional Jewish people who are not believers because they rely heavily on Orthodox religious practices—the Talmud, tradition, and works. Rabbinic Judaism is all in the minor key; even the music of traditional Judaism tends to be somber, whereas the Messianic key is joyous and vibrant, and celebrating and dancing is emblematic of us as a population. We have the beginnings of a subcultural expression that is ours and is distinctive. We're not going anywhere with this Hebrew Christian label.

"At the Council of Jerusalem, recorded in Acts 15, the discussion centered over whether Gentiles had to become Jewish to truly accept the Jewish Messiah. The decision of the early believers was clear—they did not! Yet, for almost two thousand years, Jews have been expected to drop their Jewish identities, blend into churches, and to effectively become Gentiles to accept the Jewish Messiah. This is not right, and we must reverse it and take a stand against this idea! If the Gentiles did not have to become Jews, should the Jews have to become Gentiles?"

We attempted to make our case, but the old, entrenched establishment within the Alliance did not wish to permit us to voice this innovative idea. They were determined to snuff us out at that meeting. Others of the older people could see this wasn't for them, but they

> *"Jews have been expected to drop their Jewish identities, blend into churches, and to effectively become Gentiles to accept the Jewish Messiah."*

could also see there was something to what we were saying. As well, a number of those present thought what we were saying was completely heretical.

The Vote

The time came for the vote count and it was close, just as we knew it was going to be. We all raised our hands to vote, and someone was supposed to count hands. It so happened that a number of those who were in agreement with us were all sitting together, and that row was not counted. I saw they did not count the row, presumably by accident. I was sitting right here, and they just skipped a row.

It was going to be a very close vote. The row they missed had eight or nine votes. We didn't think it was intentional; however, we wanted a recount. Even before the vote was totaled, we had our hands raised. *"Hey, you missed this row!"* But, those presiding over the conference ignored us.

Sure enough, we lost by a very few votes, but the recount would have resolved the matter in our favor. So, now we had a problem over the recount. But, the establishment—the Hebrew Christians running the conference—did *not* want to give us the recount. The question was on the agenda, and we wanted an honest vote.

I knew we had to have a recount, especially once the results were tallied and we had barely lost the count. I was immediately on my feet! *"We have to have a recount! What's to lose by taking a recount? Presumably everyone will just vote the same, correct? What's the harm?"*

"No! We're not recognizing you, Mr. Liberman!"

I wouldn't back down. I was frantically waving my hand, but they would not recognize me. *"Look! They missed a row! I'm certain of it! There has to be a recount! It's the right thing to do!"*

The outgoing president who was the chairman and moderator was just as determined to put this entire matter behind. *"Mr. Liberman, from now on, our parliamentarian will deal with you with guillotine precision!"* Everyone who was there that day remembers the words *"with guillotine precision."*

"Look! I am a dues-paying, paid-up member of this Alliance, and you have to recognize me! That's my right!"

"I'm the chairman! I can call on, or not call on, whomever I want."

I couldn't get my recount. This was a very public display and Liberman was now the goat. Everyone was blistering mad—on *both* sides!

They were *not* going to prevent us from getting our recount. I had everything at stake: my life, my family, and my congregation.

Insofar as I was concerned, the world was at stake. I would not take *no* for an answer.

So, I stood up again. *"This is of such great importance that you cannot take the rules of procedure and use them against us in a way that does not have a ring of fairness to it, especially since it is such a close vote."*

But, they did not want to recognize me.

So, I began to blurt out my case, when the parliamentarian interrupted. *"Mr. Liberman, you have to sit down or be ejected from the meeting."*

"You cannot eject me from the meeting! It would take physical force to move me out of this room! I'm asking for the recount!"

This went on until there was a break for lunch. During the lunch break, I went out and bought a copy of *Roberts Rules of Order*. When the meeting resumed after lunch, we started coming against the parliamentarian, as I waved my newly acquired copy of *Roberts Rules of Order*. *"Do you have the right to stop us from our recount? If so, explain why we are not permitted to have our recount!"* Still, they wouldn't recognize me.

I had had enough. Opinions were very heated on both sides. They were not recognizing me, and I wanted my recount. So, in front of 250 people, I trudged up onto the platform until I was within six inches of the chairman and facing him. My voice was very loud. *"Do you recognize me now? I'm standing right here in front of you. Can you now say that I'm invisible? Because I'm not leaving here, and my voice is not going to stop until you recognize me!"*

I'm having a real hissy fit. Some of the older folks looked like they were about ready to have heart attacks. Other people were renouncing me as being from the pit of Hell for causing divisiveness. It was really raucous.

Finally, they recognized me, *'Cause this guy Liberman will not shut up! The only way to shut him up is to recognize him.'* That was my intent.

"I have here a copy of Robert's Rules of Order. All right?" I'm waving the paperback over my head and pointing at it. *"You've got your parliamentarian, but I've got this book here!"*

This continued for the rest of the afternoon. Nothing made any difference. The matter was tabled with no recount. Then, we disbanded for the evening.

Some of the older folks looked like they were about ready to have heart attacks.

It was desperation on my part that compelled me to the point where I became the disruptive central figure. I was the one who had a hissy fit and wouldn't quit. I was the one who called for the recount. I was the one standing on his feet. I was the one raising his voice. I was a desperate man, but I knew I had the support of the other people. I was the one who kept insisting on the recount because, to me, ignoring the request just wasn't the right thing to do.

As far as I was concerned, this recognition of the Messianic identity had to happen. For me, it was do or die. Anything I could do physically; it had to be done. It wasn't a theoretical thing with me. It wasn't just a preference. This was a matter of the future of the congregation, and the future of the congregation had everything to do with my personal family.

I just was not taking no for an answer.

Crying Time

That night all of us Messianics got together at the motel. We were from all over the country, and we were all staying at the same motel. In the cars on the way to the motel, we were crying our guts out. Everybody was in tears and balling! This continued even after we arrived at our rooms. We were pleading with the Lord. It was as if life would end if we couldn't get this name change through.

Overnight, we collected ourselves and decided on a strategy. *"We've got to get rid of this chairman."*

Wisdom Prevails

By the next morning, everyone had cooled down. After everyone settled into their seats at the meeting hall, I raised my hand. This time, I was recognized. *"Yesterday, we had an election and Martin Chernoff was elected to be the president of the Hebrew Christian Alliance of America, but he was not seated. He should be running this meeting—not you!"*

Marty was not at all pushing his own case, but we all considered him the senior man among us who had the same vision we had for Messianic Judaism.

"Mr. Liberman, at the next conference in two years, he will be the chairman."

"I don't understand. Why does it have to wait until the next time? Shouldn't he be the chairman? Because you've already been voted out of office. You're no longer officially in office—he is. Why isn't he chairing this meeting?"

We felt we had them on this point. It was a good strategy.

A little hesitation, but the guy moved over and Martin Chernoff was in the chair. So Marty took over the meeting. Overnight, he had time to think about this entire matter. Now, Marty was chairing the meeting and things were a lot calmer. I was standing up, and he was seated. I was preparing to ask for my recount. Before I could, Marty addressed me. *"Paul, I'm going to give you your recount if you want it. You're entitled to it. What's more, there have been enough of the older folks who have left, because of the difficulty yesterday, that you'll probably win. But,*

Paul, whatever small movement we are, if you force this issue, you're going to split us in half.

"*Now, I've been thinking about this, and I have another idea. Paul, in Washington, DC, you want to be known as a Messianic Jew. How about if those cities that want to identify as Messianic Jews are free to do so, and those cities that want to identify as Hebrew Christians are free to do so? Then, in two years, at our next meeting, we will have another vote. Let's see what God does. Let's see what time does. Do you think that will be a good solution?*" I immediately recognized the truth of everything he was saying, *and the wisdom of it.*

"*I think that's a very good solution.*" So, I sat down. At last, the room was filled with consensus. All the young people who were the driving force for the name change agreed. It gave us what we wanted but didn't destroy what the others wanted. It was perfect—a choice piece of God's wisdom. Marty had *not* told us in advance about his proposed solution. Had he not been seated as president, as we requested, his solution would never have been heard.

Messianic Jewish Alliance of America

The next national Alliance meeting was held in July 1975 at Messiah College in Grantham, Pennsylvania. Once again, the resolution to change the name was brought forward and voted on. We had grown in number. By 1975, there were eight Messianic congregations throughout the USA *because* of this new Messianic identity. Also, a number of the old guard had passed away. That vote was without the intense emotions of the Dunedin, Florida conference. The name change was approved and accepted. Thereafter, the name was to be the *Messianic Jewish Alliance of America, (MJAA)*. It remains so to this day. At the same conference, I was first elected to the Executive Committee of the MJAA. In July 2011, I was elected the President of the MJAA and, as of the date of this writing, October 2014, I remain president.

From the time the name change became official, we began to grow. As of 2014, there are approximately 800 Messianic congregations worldwide including roughly 375 in the USA, and 145 congregations and home worship groups in Israel. The two largest groups are the *International Alliance of Messianic Congregations and Synagogues (IAMCS)*, a division of the MJAA with 140 affiliates, and the *Union of Messianic Jewish Congregations (UMJC)* with approximately 90 affiliates.

Hebrew Christians or Messianic Jews

The opposition to Messianic Judaism certainly did not end following the Dunedin, Florida conference. Nor, as I later found out, did it originate there.

References to this dispute are found in the minutes of the American Alliance that date back to the meetings of 1915–17. There was a tension in the earliest Alliance between Hebrew Christian and Messianic Jew. Even then, there was an incipient issue under the surface. It wasn't as though somebody within our lifetimes dreamt it up.

In 1979 or 1980, a gentleman who was about 90 years old and a Jewish believer attended our national Alliance conference in Grantham, Pennsylvania. He told us he was at the original meeting of the *Hebrew Christian Alliance of America* in 1915. Even in 1915, there was an element among the Jewish believers who wanted a more assertive sense of Jewish identity, but they were shut down. That meeting was so contentious, the police were called in to break it up. It became such a point of controversy—such a sore point—that when the Hebrew Christians won, there was a formal resolution and a vote that the subject about Messianic Jews, or Messianic Judaism, *"may never again be brought up by this Alliance."* It was a big issue then and they shut it down. They said, *"Forever, and for all time, the issue of Messianic Judaism may never be discussed—ever again!"*

But, in 1973 we were a very assertive group of young people. We were of the Jesus people generation. We were Americans who came out of the Vietnam era, the Watergate era.

Even before the 1975 vote approving the name change to the *Messianic Jewish Alliance of America*, the opposition continued to speak out against this "new" idea. Those that wanted to be identified as *"Hebrew Christian"* had very strong feelings about its continued use. They felt certain that dropping that designation would jeopardize their standing, both organizationally and individually, within their churches and denominations.

We were accused of being heretics. *"You're building a middle-wall of partition. You're putting yourself under the law. This is pride, an elitist sentiment. By being identified as Jewish believers or Messianic Jews as opposed to Hebrew Christian, you're making yourselves different. You're separating yourselves from the body."* Everywhere we went we were confronted as though we were advocating some heresy. And, so they believed. Consider a *Hebrew Christian* who's been attending a church for 25 years—is he going to be involved with these *Messianic Jews* who are not understood?

From the Council of Nicaea in 325 CE, and after, it was illegal to worship on *Shabbat*—Saturday—or to have, or attend, a Passover Seder. *"You're not supposed to be Jewish anymore. You're a former Jew. Now you're a Christian!"*

Hebrew Christians were convinced their churches and/or denominations would begin to see them with jaundiced eyes. If— in any way—they were associated with *the Messianic Jews,* they were at personal risk. Some of the missionary organizations to the Jews that received support from Christians couldn't immediately risk the change in identity. Some of these Jewish believers belonged to churches and had been doing missionary work for decades. *"Are the Messianic Jews now saying that we were doing this wrong?"* They were concerned the denominational churches would think they had gone off the deep end of the pier, and were doing something heretical.

There were two primary concerns: (1) *"This is an elitist group."* (2) *"You're putting us back under the Law."* Those were the two reservations, both of which were misperceptions. In some quarters, that same confusion still exists.

Somehow, when we were returning to things comfortably Jewish instead of singing *Onward Christian Soldiers*, and *The Old Rugged Cross*, it was very distressing. These questions were raised because we included Jewish-type things like saying the *Shema*— *"Hear O Israel, the Lord our God, the Lord is One"*—from Deuteronomy 6:4, and inserted that into the service and other similar Scripture verses that are typical Jewish things in a synagogue service, things both Scriptural *and* Jewish.

It was a departure from everything that they held as holy within the Christian Church. Of course, the Hebrew Christians weren't going to say they had made a mistake in what they had done with their lives. People will sometimes

> **Somehow, when we were returning to things comfortably Jewish instead of singing *Onward Christian Soldiers*, and *The Old Rugged Cross*, it was very distressing.**

embrace change when it is their idea. This was *not* their idea. This was at the core of the resistance we were confronting at the Dunedin, Florida conference. This left us in the opposition with most of the Jewish missions and the para-church organizations. They were against our position because they were looking for their support from the Church. Those of us who were lay people starting Messianic congregations didn't have any such concerns.

Manny Brotman was an exception. He operated a para-congregational organization, but was unconcerned with any negative blowback. Manny was pure in this regard. Otherwise, without exception, the missions organizations that were all affiliated with Christian churches and denominations were opposed to us. They were saying things about us that were clearly misperceptions. They were certainly propagating misinformation. This fed into the already suspicious parts of Christianity that viewed us with great misgiving and even considered us propagating heresy. They did not understand what we were all about.

A lot of the Jewish believers were against us, as well—especially the ones who were established teachers and leaders in churches and denominations and had ministries. They were opposed to this new *"Messianic Judaism."* Jews for Jesus took years to come around.

After the *Council of Nicaea* in 325 A.D., *true* Christians were prohibited from even having a Passover Seder. Now, we were celebrating Passover and the other biblical feasts. There were no Jewish delegates speaking up at the Council of Nicaea. For two-thousand years, to do anything Jewish was illegal and unacceptable for a follower of the Jewish Messiah; the same Jewish Messiah who, in the hours before the crucifixion, said *"I have earnestly desired to eat this Passover with you before I suffer"* (Luke 22:15). After the church councils, celebrating Passover was considered a reversion to "the Law" in the eyes of many Christians.

As our numbers began to grow, articles were written in major Christian magazines questioning, *"What are the Jewish believers doing, trying to identify as Jewish—this Messianic Jewish thing? Are they saying there's something wrong with being called Christian or that the Gentiles are something less?"*

We were a liability. It took a bunch of rebels who had nothing to lose to push this through. We were young, so we just said; *"To heck with it! We don't care what anybody thinks. We're gonna do this. Go ahead, excommunicate us. We don't care. We have nothing to lose. We never had any church affiliations to begin with. We're not church members. What can you do to us?"*

The Messianic Jewish contingency had no economic interest in the status quo. We had no jobs to safeguard. We had no standing in the Christian denominations or Christian missionary organizations. For the most part, we didn't even have Bible College or seminary educations to defend or protect. We just knew that we needed to reach the Jewish people with the Messiah and to continue with our own identities as Jews.

The Opposition

Theodor Herzl is universally recognized as the father of the modern state of Israel. In his diary, Herzl recorded two primary sources of opposition to his vision for a separate and distinct Jewish nation.

The first and most hostile adversary unexpectedly came from among the Jewish people. Herzl called them, *"the assimilationists."* This was a group of wealthy, powerful, mostly Western Jews. They had risen up through the ranks of business, the judiciary, and politics within the nations where they lived and prospered. They adamantly opposed the idea of a *"Jewish"* nation. Their stated reasons were many but boiled down to a couple of core objections.

1. If there were a Jewish nation, the "Christian" nations where the majority of the Jews lived would feel justified in "encouraging," if not forcibly expelling, their Jewish citizens, requiring them to relocate to the new Jewish state.

2. The loyalty of the Jewish citizens among the Western nations would be challenged, questioned, and attacked. The presumption was that the Jews' primary "allegiance" would be to the Jewish nation, not to the place of their birth, education, and business.

33—Christians or Jews?

The "assimilationists" argued that there was no need for a Jewish state. Their personal achievements proved it was possible for Jews to thrive, even among Christians in a Christian nation.

Herzl believed that many of this group would have gladly cast off all distinguishing, identifying marks as Jews, were it possible; and in fact, he believed that was the assimilationist's ultimate goal—if not for themselves, then for their children.

The second major source of opposition Herzl reported came from among the Gentiles—*the anti-Semites*. This second group roundly opposed any creation of a new, modern nation–state composed of a Jewish population. They fought it at every opportunity. For example, even after the adoption of the Balfour Declaration by Great Britain in 1917, the British anti-Semites thwarted every attempted implementation of the promised Jewish nation. It took the exodus of Britain from Palestine in 1948 for Israel to be born.

Likewise, the growth of the modern Messianic Jewish revival was a bone in the throat of a significant voice within Gentile Christian theology—a contradiction of their settled doctrine that there would only be a revival among the Jews *after* the Tribulation began. That's the way they saw it. For others, a more virulent group of anti-Semites could not be found than those who held, and do hold, to "Replacement Theology"; the certain conviction that God has ceased, forever, to deal with the Jewish people and Israel. According to this doctrine, all of the promises have passed to the (Gentile) Church. Of course, the Jews retain the curses.

I regret to say, this anti-Semitism—sometimes in the guise of *anti-Zionism*—is on the rise among a number of major Christian denominations. Too often, the Messianic Jewish movement is found to be an obstacle to historic, theological preconceptions.

But we're here, and we're not leaving, at least not until our Messiah takes us.

Epilogue—Flip of the Coin

It was the summer of 1970: my first trip with Charlie Barr to Washington, DC. The two of us had come from Chicago with the goal of identifying a career opportunity for me through one of Charlie's many political contacts. After I was interviewed and hired at the Commerce Department, we drove our rental car back to the airport prior to our return flight.

"Paul, now things are going to spring into action. You're going to have to relocate."

"So, Charlie, I've been doing some research, and I understand there are basically two possible areas to think about— suburban Maryland and suburban Virginia. What do you think? Which would be the better choice for my family?"

Charlie considered the trade-offs for a minute. *"That's a good question. You're Jewish, and Maryland has a significant Jewish population that would be good for you socially. But, that area of Maryland tends to be quite liberal. On the other hand, Virginia tends to be conservative and has been electing conservative candidates."*

"What do you think, Charlie? Which would be better?"

"Paul, I have difficulty advising you on this. It's really the flip of a coin. You have to decide."

"All right, Charlie, maybe that is the way to decide—the flip of a coin."

By the time I made this trip with Charlie to Washington, DC, I was already taken with the idea of destiny. In my mind, it made perfect sense. *'Let destiny decide!'*

Charlie pulled a quarter out of his pocket. *"You call it, Paul. If it turns up heads, it's Maryland. If it's tails, it's Northern Virginia."*

Epilogue—Flip of the Coin

The quarter came up tails. As it turned out, that simple coin toss sealed my life's decision to move to Northern Virginia. That's where I met Ray McCauley on the bus ride to work—the man who gave me the booklet that changed my life. Years later, I can't help but wonder: '*What would have happened had the coin gone the other way?*'

Or, what if my twelve-year-old grandfather in Minsk had not missed his father in New York so much that he forged a letter telling the entire Liberman clan to leave Belarus and move to New York City?

Eventually, I came to understand who is behind destiny. *He* had a destiny for me. Even before I was born, He was operating to bring about that destiny.

And, *He has a destiny for you!*

Parting Words

Jewish—Not Yet a Believer

If you're Jewish and have not yet accepted the claims of the New Testament, this book was written for you. Many of the questions and objections Paul Liberman wrestled with have no doubt resonated with you.

The God of our fathers—Abraham, Isaac, and Jacob—is loving and patient. Reach out to Him in honesty and sincerity, expressing your need and desire for the Truth. He will not disappoint you. Take a look at the "Parking Lot Prayer"—Appendix "A"—which is modeled after Paul's own prayer when he originally reached out to Messiah Yeshua.

Find a New Testament and read it for yourself. Some suggestions for good, modern translations can be found in "For Additional Information"— Appendix "B." Don't take someone else's word regarding the content of this important book. Read it and draw your own conclusion, while whispering a prayer to the God of your fathers to reveal the Truth—whatever it is! *No one should ever fear the Truth.*

The authors have also provided a list of websites also included in "For Additional Information"— Appendix "B." When Paul first embraced the Messiah, he had difficulties locating other Jewish believers who shared his new faith. Today, this is no longer an issue. Jews who accept Yeshua as the son of David and promised Messiah of Israel, live in every country where Jews live, including Israel. Reach out to any one of them and they will help you with your questions. A number can be contacted through the websites provided in the Appendix.

Fundamentalist Evangelical Christian

The overwhelming majority of Christians do not have a clue what the historic and cultural barriers are which separate the Jewish people from the Jewish Messiah. If you have read this book, you are now among a small percentage of informed Christians who now "gets it."

The most important role we have as a follower of the Jewish Messiah, is to pass on our faith to those who do not yet share in our great hope—the free gift of eternal life.

If you have read this book, it is no doubt because you already possess a love for the Jewish people. Studies reveal between 80%-90% of first generation Jewish believers initially considered the claims of the Messiah and the New Testament after a discussion or interaction with a Gentile Christian. (A "first generation" Jewish believer is a person whose Jewish parents and grandparents were not believers.) Paul Liberman's story is an illustration of this point.

You can assist in reaching first generation Jewish believers and help shape the future. 1) Make a list of every Jewish neighbor, co-worker, classmate, and business associate. Don't forget your dentist, your banker, and your professor. 2) Purchase a gift copy of this book for each person on your list. You can do this at www.DontCallMeChristian.com. Use the coupon code—TO THE JEW FIRST—to get two free copies for each copy you purchase at retail; that's three for the price of one. We are making these books available so that you can purchase as many as required to distribute to every Jewish person on your list.

A single book given by Ray McCauley changed the life and direction of Paul Liberman. Paul's life has had an impact on countless more Jewish lives. *"How will they hear unless someone tells them?"*

Jewish Believer

If you are Jewish and have already embraced Messiah Yeshua, you should personally identify with the story of Paul Liberman. Perhaps you have close friends and family who don't understand the direction your life has taken. They certainly don't understand your faith.

This book provides you a perfect opportunity to bridge the gap of misunderstanding. Every reservation and objection your family and friends have expressed has been addressed within Paul's story—this book. 1) Make a list of every adult family member and Jewish friend. 2) Purchase a copy of this book for everyone on your list. You can do this at www.DontCallMeChristian.com. Use the coupon code—TO THE JEW FIRST—to get two free copies for each single copy you purchase; that's three for the price of one. We are making these books available so that you can purchase as many as required to distribute to every Jewish family member, associate, and friend on your list.

They still might not agree with you after reading this book, but they *will* understand you. Most importantly, they will know that embracing faith in the Jewish Messiah does not result in the loss of Jewish identity. You haven't become a Gentile or embraced a Gentile religion. What could be *more* Jewish than to accept a Jewish Messiah, the son of David, prophesied in the Jewish Holy Scriptures, who was born, lived and died in the Jewish land— the Jewish Messiah who changed the entire history of the World?

Parking Lot Prayer—Appendix A

If you are a typical Jewish person, it is not difficult to relate to Paul Liberman's story. Perhaps you read this book out of curiosity, or because a neighbor or relative gave it to you and you were just being courteous.

If you are ready for a personal relationship with the God of your fathers—Abraham, Isaac, and Jacob—that is possible, right now. He has not changed since He first spoke to Abraham and, more than anything, he wants to have that same connection with you. He will help. All He requires from you is your permission. This is possible when you invite Him into your heart and life.

Prayer is speaking to Him. Pour out your heart in private to the God who hears. Recall Paul's prayer as he paced back and forth in that Washington, DC parking lot on his lunch break. It's a model for any Jewish person. The Parking Lot Prayer changed Paul Liberman's life forever, and it can also change yours. While Paul paced, he spoke out loud to God.

"God, I'm very confused about all this. Is this Gentile propaganda, or is it the truth? I'm very confused about it, and I don't know what's going to clarify it for me because I can't really discuss it with anybody. If you are God, You ought to be able to straighten out my confusion. You have to help me out here.

"And, as regards all this Jesus business—if this Yeshua/Jesus is the Messiah—if he is the Messiah and the answer to all these prophecies, I need a Messiah for my situation, and I need him right away. I want him to be my Messiah. Okay? Cause, the way it looks to me, nobody can help me except a Messiah. Take over—however it works, take over."

After he prayed the Parking Lot Prayer, remember what Paul said. *"If He can't hear that, He can't hear anything and there's no point ever praying at all for anything. If He does answer my prayer, then okay. Now I've got some kind of a foundation going here. This is a win-win situation."*

For Additional Information—Appendix B

In 1971, at the time Paul Liberman first began to explore the subject of the New Testament and the Jewish Messiah, it was difficult. Today, there are many opportunities to directly engage with other Jewish people, even Rabbis, who have made this same spiritual journey. There are Jewish believers living in every country in the world in which Jews reside. Messianic Jewish congregations are in many of the world's largest cities, as well as many out of the way locations. The internet makes it possible to research these matters in the privacy of your own home, apartment, or dorm room with the aid of your computer.

For your convenience, we have included here a list of some websites that will assist you in your investigation and will help you to connect with someone personally or by email. This list is by no means comprehensive, but it will assist you in your search effort. The list is in no particular order. No one should ever be apprehensive while making a sincere search for the Truth. Only a lie fears the Truth.

General Information: Just Looking

It's a lot to take in. We get it. Included here is a sample of organizations and individuals who understand the questions a Jewish person has about the Messiah and the New Testament.

http://www.isaiah53.com/

http://www.chosenpeople.com

http://www.jewishvoice.org/

http://www.jewsforjesus.org/

(From LSD to PhD—Messianic Jew, Dr. Michael Brown)

https://www.youtube.com/watch?v=icJ0T0XcJMQ

http://askdrbrown.org/

Dr. Michael Brown's daily broadcast
http://www.lineoffireradio.com/

http://ffoz.org/messiah/journal/

http://www.realmessiah.com/

324 Messianic Prophecies

http://www.apostolic-ministries.net/324_messianic_prophecies.pdf

http://thekingsjewishvoice.org/

http://sidroth.org/

http://mjbi.org

http://www.sandrasheskinbrotman.com/

http://olivepresspublishing.org/messianic-books.html

http://www.jewishjewels.org/

http://ariel.org/

http://cjfm.org/

http://rabbierict.com/

http://messianicjewish.net/about

(Israel)

http://www.maozisrael.org

http://www.tikkunministries.org/

http://loveisrael.org/

http://www.israeltoday.co.il/

(Brazil)

http://www.debrandinggod.org/

Most of the above sources are English language. However, there is lots of information in other languages. For example:

(Hebrew)

www.think4yourself.co.il

https://www.youtube.com/HEAROISRAEL7

(Russian)

www.think4yourself.ru

The New Testament

When a Jewish person like Paul Liberman, begins to think "outside the box" with regard to the subject of the Jewish Messiah, he or she must read the New Testament. For many, like Paul, there is apprehension mixed with the knowledge that the investigation is personal. Cultural and historic strictures cannot prevent honest research.

When Paul sought out his first copy of the New Testament, he visited the Library of Congress on his lunch break. At that time, there were only a handful of translations apart from the King James Version.

Today, a number of very good options are readily available— accurate translations into modern English, all of which also include the Holy Scriptures, the Tenach. Here are a couple of recommendations.

Tree of Life Messianic Bible translation. For information visit: www.treeoflifebible.org

Modern English Version translation. For information visit http://modernenglishversion.com/

Complete Jewish Bible translation. For information visit: https://www.biblegateway.com/versions/Complete-Jewish-Bible-CJB/

New American Standard Bible translation. For information visit:
http://www.lockman.org/

Messianic Jewish Congregations

Today there are congregations of Jewish believers in many nations throughout the world. The following are a few examples:

Messianic Jewish Alliance of America (MJAA). For information visit: http://www.mjaa.org/

Union of Messianic Jewish Congregations (UMJC). For information visit: http://www.umjc.org/

International Alliance of Messianic Congregations and Synagogues (IAMCS). http://www.iamcs.org/

Website for Directory of Israeli Messianic Congregations: http://www.yeshuasharvest.org/living-stones/connecting-with-believers/directory-of-israeli-congregation

The Association of Messianic Congregations http://www.messianicassociation.org/

Connect International

International Messianic Jewish Alliance (IMJA). For information visit: www.IMJA.org

Union of British Messianic Synagogues http://www.ubmsonline.org/

Israel Study: http://www.israelcollege.com/

Russia: For information visit: http://mjbi.org/Russia/

Also http://kehilatyeshua.narod.ru/english.html

Eastern Europe: http://www.reachinitiative.com/

About Paul Liberman—Appendix C

Paul Liberman accepted the Jewish Messiah in 1971. He was instrumental in founding two Messianic Congregations: Beth Messiah Messianic Congregation–Washington, DC and Tree of Life–San Diego, California. He also served as a congregational leader at Beit Asaph–Netanya, Israel, while residing in Israel. He and Susan, his wife, received Israeli citizenship in 1991.

During his years residing in Israel, he was a founder of The Joseph Project—an NGO (Non-Governmental Organization) providing humanitarian aid in Israel. He was elected Executive Director of the Messianic Action Committee, a political action committee lobbying the Israeli government in opposition of legislation negatively impacting Messianic Jews and Christians in Israel.

Paul served as the Executive Director of the IMJA (International Messianic Jewish Alliance) for five years. The IMJA is an alliance of Messianic Jewish believers representing 16 nations on five continents.

For six years, Paul operated as the publisher of "The Messianic Times," a newspaper representing the Messianic Jewish community worldwide. He is a founding board member of MAOZ, Inc. (Israel). He presently serves as the congregational leader of Ohav Shalom Messianic Congregation, Palm Springs, California. As of 2015, Paul is the President of the MJAA (Messianic Jewish Alliance of America). Paul and his wife, Susan, hold dual citizenship in the United States and Israel.

Career Profile

Paul Liberman is a successful small business entrepreneur and turnaround specialist. From a beginning in purchasing and sales for the Liberman family electrical supply business, Chicago,

Illinois, he launched into political campaigning and fund-raising for national Senatorial and Congressional candidates.

This resulted in a position in the U.S. Commerce Department, in Washington, DC, where he became a Director of Congressional Relations. As a sideline, Paul's productive personal investment efforts led to his becoming a licensed securities dealer and syndicator, packaging investments through the firm he founded—Madison Investment Properties, Inc.

Following the profitable sale of Madison Investment Properties, Paul started an American subsidiary of a foreign multinational firm, leading to a relocation in 1984 to San Diego, California, where he also purchased a company out of bankruptcy, restoring it to profitability.

With the sale of that business in 1994, Paul moved to Israel and became a 50% owner of an Israeli import/export business, which he also proceeded to turn around to operational profitability. After nine years living in Israel, Paul sold his interest and relocated back to Southern California. There he joined A.G. Edwards—the national investment firm—as a Securities Broker. Subsequent to his return from Israel, he was asked to accomplish a turnaround for two non-profit organizations, which he successfully accomplished.

In 1964, Mr. Liberman received a Bachelor of Science degree in Economics from the University of Wisconsin. In 2001, he received his Master's degree in Business Administration from Washington International University, Washington, DC after completing a thesis in International Banking and Finance. His thesis compared Central Bank policies in various nations.

Family Background

Paul and Susan Liberman were born of Jewish parents and grandparents. They come from traditional mid-western

American Jewish homes and backgrounds. They have been married for 50 years.

Their sons, Joel and Evan Liberman, were raised with a high respect for their Jewish heritage and had a Bar Mitzvah. Joel, the older, became a Certified Public Accountant (CPA) and has a rabbinical ordination. He and his wife, Darcie, have two children and reside in San Diego, where Joel leads Tree of Life Messianic Congregation, originally founded by Paul in 1987.

Evan has a degree in Computer Science from University of California, Santa Barbara. He and his wife, Sarah, reside in Israel and are Israeli citizens. They have three Israeli children. After 20 years employed in high tech with major firms, Evan pursued a career as a registered securities broker, International investment advisor and portfolio manager.

Public Affairs Experience

Illinois

1968–69: Campaign Manager, Illinois Constitutional convention–prevailed over eleven other candidates.

1969–70: Illinois State Assembly–Slated as Republican Candidate.

Regional Director, U.S. Senatorial Campaign Staff–Senator Ralph Smith (Illinois)–Greater Chicago Metro area.

Midwest Finance Committee–Executive Director for Conservative candidates U.S. Senators, Paul Fannin (Arizona), Ted Stevens (Alaska) and Congressman Clark McGregor for Senate (Minnesota).

Executive Director, Advisory Council–Illinois Governor Richard Ogilvie.

Washington, DC

1971–78: Planner/Coordinator, White House Conference *The Industrial World Ahead in 1990.*

Attendees included President Richard Nixon, Cabinet members of Nixon

White House, National Labor Union leaders and 500 national corporate Presidents and CEO's.

Director of Congressional Relations–U.S. Commerce Department. Monitored the approximately 1,500 business bills annually introduced. From these, tracked, reported on, and/or actively lobbied in behalf of 150.

USA

1979–93: Public Relations Advisor/Consultant, non–profit Jewish and Israel Charities. Board membership of National and International Israel Advocacy organizations. Created and/or stimulated and consolidated local community public opinion groups—Maryland, Virginia, Pennsylvania, Massachusetts, New York, and California.

Israel

1995–99: Lobbied Israeli Knesset–Religious Rights issues. Joined with the political parties—Likud (center right) and Meretz (liberal left)—to oppose far right Shas Rabbinical Party. Succeeded in defeating oppressive legislation which would have resulted in serious curtailment of religious freedom in Israel, and the imposition of criminal penalties including substantial fines and prison sentences for religious dissidents and non-conformists.

2000–03: Executive Director–Non-profit Humanitarian Aid Importer, the Joseph Project. Successfully obtained exclusive license for the purpose of importing humanitarian aid into Israel. Through the end of 2014, over $100 million aid had been delivered by the Joseph Project.

California

2010–2013: Tea Party Patriots Coalition–Palm Springs, CA.

2012–present: Finance Committee Member–RNC (Republican National Committee)

2012–Romney Battleground Fund Investor

2012–Finance Committee, Orange County, CA–Romney/Ryan Presidential Campaign

2013–present: Board of Governors–Council for National Policy

About Jack Wasson—Appendix D

Jack Wasson graduated summa cum laude in 1979 from the University of Texas, Arlington, with three bachelor's degrees including History (Modern European), Political Science (International), and Psychology (Behavioral). He served in the Army as an officer in Military Intelligence. In 1972, he first graduated from Southwestern Assemblies of God Bible College, Waxahachie, Texas. Since 1981 he has operated as an independent businessman, Real Estate Broker, and General Contractor in both Texas and California. He has owned and operated businesses in real estate and oil development, construction and finance. Jack has been affiliated with the Messianic Jewish movement since 1972. He currently serves on the Administrative Committee of the IMJA (International Messianic Jewish Alliance). He has traveled on multiple occasions to Europe and Israel. He writes for the Jacob Report (www.JacobReport.com). His complete biography is available on the Jacob Report website. This is his second book. In 2015, he is 67 years old.

About The Book Cover—Appendix E

Those are NOT stars! They are Galaxies! Every one of those points of light is an individual Galaxy, each one consisting of from 100 million to a trillion stars! The cover "background" is the Hubble Deep Field photo which was taken in order to estimate the number of Galaxies in the visible Universe! The calculated answer—about 500 billion total Galaxies!

Through Abraham, all the nations of the world were to be blessed. The Blessed Messiah of Israel was the gift of God to the entire world. Yeshua confirmed He is the Light of the World. Scripture says Messiah is the Light of the World and that God dwells in unapproachable light.

So Messiah is the light shining forth from Israel (light emanating from the Star of David). This Light is brighter than ANY light in the Universe for the Light of God is uncreated, while all the light of all the stars in all the galaxies of the Universe is created light! That's the meaning of the cover.

Acknowledgements

In February, 2013, Jack Wasson, a close personal friend, broached the idea of recording my life story as a keepsake record for my grandchildren. From the first interview session, we mutually recognized that the story had implications beyond the Liberman family. Our change of purpose to accommodate a larger audience required transferring numerous hours of recorded interviews into manuscript form. Jack and I wish to express our gratitude to those who tackled what was, at times, a daunting task and who co-labored with us in producing this book.

Rochelle Phillips did a heroic job of transcribing the many digital recordings. Anyone who has attempted this knows it is a laborious task. Gail Levin served as transcript editor, listening to each of the recordings and filling in the gaps on the transcriptions. Her Jewish background proved invaluable in catching the phrasing of Jewish terms and names that might otherwise be lost in translation. Gail also did an excellent job of editing our rough draft, ensuring the transition from transcript to manuscript read naturally and smoothly.

A special word of appreciation to my son, Joel, who read countless rewrites of individual chapters, always providing encouragement and many valuable comments.

We owe a great deal of gratitude to Dianne, who put the professional editor's polish on the final manuscript, lending her expertise and that "extra set of eyes" that is so invaluable. Her questions and comments from the perspective of a Christian with very little knowledge of Jewish culture or Messianic believers was invaluable, insuring that we were "communicating."

Each person worked diligently on their assigned part and together helped us transform raw interviews into what we believe is a truly professional product.

Acknowledgements

Our special thanks to Daniel Savart, who did the cover graphics. He took a concept Jack could only see in his head and transformed a vision into a reality.

Jack and I want to acknowledge his lovely wife, Constance, for allowing Jack to take a year from "productive business" to work on this project.

Our sincerest appreciation to Steve Strang, President and Founder of Charisma Media, and his team who reviewed the manuscript and assured us of the quality of the final product.

We also appreciate those who took the time to review a pre-publication copy, providing personal words of encouragement and many valuable "tweaks" that were included in the final copy, including Jonathan Bernis, Mitch Glaser, Sid Roth, David Brickner, Susan Pearlman, Pat Robertson, Dr. George Wood, and Jack Hayford.

Particular recognition is owed to Shira Sorko-Ram, who marked up the entire prepublication version and made countless comments and edits, about 70% of which made it to the final copy. Thank you, Shira, for your years of support and friendship.

PAUL LIBERMAN

Reorder This Book!

Additional copies of **DON'T CALL ME CHRISTIAN** are available at special quantity discounts for bulk purchase of copies intended for distribution purposes. For details, go to the book website at **www.DontCallMeChristian.com**

Buy One, Get Two Free! Coupon Here!

The authors believe this story focuses on the most important Jewish issue: the spiritual purpose and meaning of our life. In order to facilitate the widest possible distribution of this book within the Jewish community, for every book you buy at retail, we will send you two additional copies for free! When you order from the website, punch in the coupon code—TO THE JEW FIRST.

Make a list of all of your Jewish friends and relatives, then go to **www.DontCallMeChristian.com** and take advantage of this opportunity! Jewish professionals as well your classmates, professors, and your neighbors all face the same concerns and might appreciate this book as a gift. And, don't forget your local Rabbi! (He should *definitely* be aware of this book!)